LISTENING
A D V A N C E D

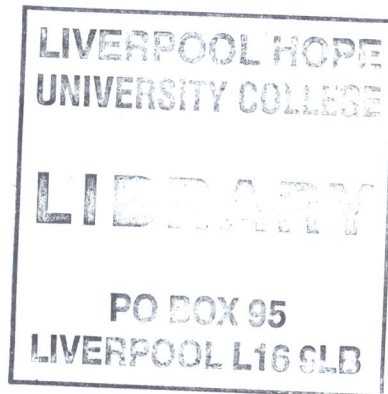

JANE REVELL
& BARRY BREARY

LISTENING
A D V A N C E D

O X F O R D   S U P P L E M E N T A R Y   S K I L L S

SERIES EDITOR: ALAN MALEY

OXFORD UNIVERSITY PRESS

Oxford University Press
Walton Street, Oxford OX2 6DP

Oxford New York Toronto Madrid
Delhi Bombay Calcutta Madras Karachi
Kuala Lumpur Singapore Hong Kong Tokyo
Nairobi Dar es Salaam Cape Town
Melbourne Auckland

and associated companies in
Berlin Ibadan

Oxford and *Oxford English* are trade marks of
Oxford University Press

ISBN 0 19 453422 7

© Oxford University Press 1988

First published 1988
Fifth impression 1993

Set by Tradespools Ltd, Frome, Somerset

Printed in Hong Kong

CONTENTS

FOREWORD

This series covers the four skill areas of Listening, Speaking, Reading and Writing at four levels—elementary, intermediate, upper-intermediate and advanced. Although we have decided to retain the traditional division of language use into the 'four skills', the skills are not treated in total isolation. In any given book the skill being dealt with serves as the *focus* of attention and is always interwoven with and supported by other skills. This enables teachers to concentrate on skills development without losing touch with the more complex reality of language use.

Our authors have had in common the following principles, that material should be:

- creative—both through author-creativity leading to interesting materials, and through their capacity to provoke creative responses from students;
- interesting—both for their cognitive and affective content, and for the activities required of the learners;
- fluency-focused—bringing in accuracy work only in so far as it is necessary to the completion of an activity;
- task-based—rather than engaging in closed exercise activities, to use tasks with pay-offs for the learners;
- problem-solving focused—so as to engage students in cognitive effort and thus provoke meaningful interaction;
- humanistic—in the sense that the materials speak to and interrelate with the learners as real people and engage them in interaction grounded in their own experience.
- learning-centred—by ensuring that the materials promote learning and help students to develop their own strategies for learning. This is in opposition to the view that a pre-determined content is taught and identically internalized by all students. In our materials we do not expect input to equal intake.

By ensuring continuing consultation between and among authors at different levels, and by piloting the materials, the levels have been established on a pragmatic basis. The fact that the authors, between them, share a wide and varied body of experience has made this possible without losing sight of the need to pitch materials and tasks at an attainable level while still allowing for the spice of challenge.

There are three main ways in which these materials can be used:

- as a supplement to a core course book;
- as self-learning material. Most of the books can be used on an individual basis with a minimum of teacher guidance, though the interactive element is thereby lost.
- as modular course material. A teacher might, for instance, combine intermediate *Listening and Speaking* books with upper-intermediate *Reading* and elementary *Writing* with a class which had a good passive knowledge of English but which needed a basic grounding in writing skills.

These materials (a book and two cassettes) are intended for adults and young adults learning English at post-First Certificate/pre-Proficiency level. They consist of ten units of varying length, each with a central topic or theme. Each unit has one or more listening passages and introduces or revises several listening skills (see the Map of the book on pages ix and x) and provides activities which promote practice of these skills. A Key to closed questions is included at the back of the book as are transcripts of the recordings.

INTRODUCTION TO THE TEACHER

Using the materials

The units can be worked through in the order presented or they can be used more flexibly. You can select a unit by choosing a topic that interests your students, or you can decide on a specific skill they want to develop (say, listening for specific information), and work through the relevant parts of the units which practise that skill. It is not essential to work through each unit from beginning to end. Select those parts that you think your students will find most useful and enjoyable.

Aims of the materials

The materials are designed to do the following:

1 to show students that they can learn to feel at ease with authentic English of the sort that they might encounter on the radio, or in an overheard conversation, talk or interview.
2 to help students develop the strategies and skills necessary for dealing with such types of spoken material.

The listening texts

The recorded material is, with one exception, authentic/unscripted and an attempt has been made to provide a variety of text types including interviews, monologues, conversations and a song. A variety of speakers have been recorded including children, older people and speakers with different accents. Transcripts of the recordings are printed at the back of the book and it is hoped that students will be encouraged to follow up some of the listening tasks by further listening with the transcript in front of them.

Skills and activities

Skills such as listening to construct a context, listening for the main idea, and listening for specific information are introduced and revised throughout the book. A wide variety of activities is also provided ranging from gap-filling and comprehension questions through information-transfer and problem-solving to much wider discussion activities.

In some activities students are encouraged to express their own opinions and preferences. In others—the prediction activities and questionnaires, for example—they are encouraged to use their own knowledge and experience. Here, it is *not* important that students know all the answers to all of the questions and predict accurately. What *is* important is that they be given a chance to think about issues *before* they listen to something, because this gives them a reason for listening and therefore facilitates the subsequent tasks. (A word of warning: be careful not to let prediction activities take up too much of the lesson and be prepared to cut them completely if you discover that none of your students knows anything at all about the topic!)

All of the units contain a lot of speaking activities as well as some reading (and occasionally writing) activities. This is because we feel that these skills do not occur, nor should they be taught, in isolation and also because a diet of pure listening would become monotonous. All the activities, however, relate directly to the listening topics and are designed to aid the development of listening skills.

For those activities which involve using new vocabulary (e.g. Unit 6 Section 1 Task 3) we would suggest that students work in groups and look up the unknown vocabulary in a learner's monolingual dictionary.

A final word

These materials are based on the belief that students—particularly at post-intermediate level and beyond—need and want to listen to interesting and informative materials as well as do challenging tasks to develop their listening skills. By listening to and talking about things which are important, and which they can relate to, they are likely both to learn something new and develop their listening skills better and faster.

MAP OF THE BOOK

Unit	Title	Listening texts	Listening skills practised	Topic/theme
1	Frightfully super	1 Conversation (four people) 2 Song 3 Interview with songwriter	Listening to construct a context Listening for the speaker's viewpoint and attitude Predicting information using clues of context, rhythm and rhyme Listening for detail Listening for specific information	How people communicate and how they listen – or don't listen – to one another
2	Does it have to be grim?	1 Interview with a doctor from the Health Education Council 2 Interview with famous octogenarian, Barbara Cartland	Listening for specific information Listening for the main idea Listening for detail	Looking after yourself and keeping fit
3	For everything!	1 Group of children talking about reading 2 Teacher talking about the value of reading (American) 3 Interviews with two famous authors of children's books (British and American)	Listening to construct a context Listening for specific information Listening for key words Listening for the main idea	Children and reading – reasons for encouraging it, what makes a popular children's book
4	Genre	1 Seven pieces of music 2 Discussion (two people) of a certain genre of film	Listening to construct a context Listening and associating ideas (excerpts from film soundtracks) Listening for the main ideas Listening for detail	The cinema – and one genre of film in particular
5	Bulletins	1 Eight excerpts from radio news bulletins 2 Four stories from radio news 3 Traffic bulletin 4 Tuning in a radio across several stations 5 Three bulletins about transport accidents	Listening for the main idea Predicting structural and lexical content from context Listening for specific information Listening for the main idea	Information broadcasts, typical of British radio

Unit	Title	Listening texts	Listening skills practised	Topic/theme
6	Medicine matters	1 Interview with a diabetic and a specialist nurse 2 Interview with trainee acupuncturist (New Zealander)	Listening to construct a context Listening for specific information Listening for the main ideas	Diabetes and its management Holistic v. conventional medicine
7	Diamond demand	Interview with an investigative journalist (American)	Listening for the main ideas Listening for detail Listening for specific information	Myths and realities of the international diamond trade
8	Flying around freely	Extended interview with an entymologist and manager of a butterfly farm	Listening to construct a context Listening for specific information Listening with the transcript Listening for the main idea	The concept and contents of a butterfly farm
9	Egypt for the day	1 Eleven extracts describing stages of the journey 2 Interviews with six people describing the journey 3 Pilot's answers to an interviewer's questions (questions edited out) 4 Interviewer's questions – isolated for stress and intonation practice 5 Complete recording of day's events of which 1–4 are extracts	Listening to construct a context Listening to identify specific words and phrases Listening for specific information Listening for detail Listening to identify phonological features	A day trip to Cairo on Concorde
10	Throwing the voice – catching the drift	1 Extracts from sixteen speeches (American) 2 Car advertisement 3 Five extracts from conversations 4 Compilation: a poem, extract from a radio play, a car advertisement, a station announcement	Listening to identify functions Listening for detail Listening to identify speaker's mood and attitude	A brief look at how choice of language, voice type and phonological features affect our understanding of a speaker's message and mood

ACKNOWLEDGEMENTS

The authors would like to thank the following people for their help in the preparation of this book: Margaret Meneses and the children of InterAlumina School, Ciudad Guayana, Venezuela; colleagues and students in Ciudad Guayana and Bilbao.

Acknowledgements are also made to the following individuals or organizations which have allowed us to use material which falls within their copyright: The British Butterfly Conservation Society; Jonathan Cape Ltd for an extract from *The Enormous Crocodile* by Roald Dahl (illustrated by Quentin Blake); The Health Education Council, London; The London Diamond Centre; *The Observer*; Rene Wyndham.

Illustrations by:

David Birdsall
Caroline Della Porta
Camilla Jessel
Jeremy Moeran
Laura Simmonds.

Photographs reproduced by permission of:

Allsport
Camera Press
Colorific
Hutchison Library
The Ronald Grant Archive
Kobal Collection
The London Diamond Centre
Rex Features
SATOUR.

1

Frightfully super

1 Making polite noises

Task 1   Listening for context

Listen to the conversation and try to decide:

where the people are
what they're doing
who they are and what their relationship is
what they're talking about.

Task 2   Using clues

Write down in the table below the clues you used—noises or words—to reach your decisions in Task 1

Setting (where)	Event (what)	People and relationships	Topic

Compare your ideas with a partner's.

Task 3   Discussion

In groups, tell each other about the last time you were in a similar situation.

- Were you the host or a guest?
- Who else was there?
- What sort of food did you eat?
- Can you remember what you talked about?
- Did you enjoy yourself or not? Why?
- Do you normally enjoy giving and/or going to dinner parties? What does it depend on?

2 Dinner parties

Task 1   Recognizing viewpoint and attitude

Listen to the song called 'Dinner parties', written, arranged and sung by Rene Wyndham.

- What does the speaker feel about dinner parties and why?
- Why does she say they are 'frightfully super'? What exactly does she mean?

Task 2   Discussion

Is the singer's attitude similar or different to yours? Discuss your views with a partner.

Task 3   Predicting content

Look at the words of the song below and on page 4. The fourth and eighth lines have been omitted from every verse. Can you write them in?
Note: Use the rhythm and rhyme of the song to help you, as well as the context and overall meaning.

DINNER PARTIES

1   Good evening, it's so kind of you
    To have us here tonight.
    We didn't feel like coming

    ....

    My word! You really do look well,
    And younger every year.
    I feel I have to say that

    ....

Chorus
Dinner parties are frightfully super.
Play your cards well and it's all fun and games.
Dinner parties are frightfully super.
Meet the right people and drop the right names.

2 Your children have grown up so fast.
They change each time we come.
They look really intelligent,

....

The little girl's just like her mum.
The boy's just like his dad.
If they keep growing up like this,

....

3 The coq au vin was quite superb.
It tasted like old hen.
I'd never had your cheesecake,

....

I couldn't stand your homemade wine
So I left it in the cup.
Could you pass me the recipe for your ratatouille?

....

4 The conversation really flowed,
At least *you* never stopped.
We couldn't get a word in

....

The evening was quite splendid
We've not laughed so much in years
I'm sorry, we really must go now

....

Task 4   Listening for detail

Listen to the song again in order to check what you wrote in Task 3.

Task 5

Divide the verses of the song (not the chorus) into two parts,
according to what the singer *thinks* when she's at a dinner party, and
what she actually *says*.

3 Do people communicate?

Task 1   Predicting content

Below are some questions (some of which have been rephrased) that
an interviewer asked Rene Wyndham. Can you predict the sort of
answers she might give in each case?

- How did you come to write the song?
- Why don't people ask direct questions?
- Do people really listen to one another? If not, why not?
- What themes do you write about in your other songs?
- Why do you write songs rather than anything else?

Discuss your predictions with other students.

Rene Wyndham

Task 2   Listening for specific information

Listen to the interview with Rene Wyndham and find out what
answers she actually gave to the questions you have just been
considering. Note: you may find it helpful to write down some of the
key words as you listen.

Are her answers very different from your predictions?

Task 3   Discussion

Discuss the following questions with other students:

- Which of the things Rene says do you agree with? Why?
- Which of the things she says do you disagree with? Why?
- Do you enjoy talking about more personal issues in your English
  classes? Why/Why not?
- What sort of things do you want to talk about?

Task 4   Language recap

Without referring back to the transcript of the song or the interview,
try to match words in the first column with ones in the second column
to make expressions, e.g. *small talk*.

Discuss with other students what the expressions mean, and give an
example of how they are used.

1 small	a face
2 fun and	b games
3 bored to	c names
4 polite	d talk
5 drop	e tears
6 pluck up	f the mark
7 miss	g noises
8 lose	h the issue
9 skirt	i courage

2

Does it have to be grim?

1 The 's' factors

How much do you know about keeping fit? This questionnaire may give you a few surprises! Tick one choice for each question, and then compare your answers with those of other students.

So you think you know how to look after yourself

1 Keeping fit is important

☐ a especially for people who lead an active life

☐ b especially for people who sit around doing nothing

☐ c for everybody, whatever their lifestyle

☐ d for everybody who wants to keep in shape.

2 Regular exercise can build up your strength, develop your stamina and keep you supple. Which is more important for protecting your heart and arteries?

☐ a strength

☐ b stamina

☐ c suppleness

☐ d All three are equally important.

3 Here are four forms of exercise. Assuming you do it regularly, which one is best for developing staying power?

☐ a vigorous swimming

☐ b yoga

☐ c weight-lifting

☐ d golf

4 The best type of exercise is something which

☐ a is enjoyable enough to keep doing on a long term basis

☐ b is irksome and arduous and gives you a sense of achievement

☐ c really stretches your muscles and even hurts a little

☐ d is really energetic and totally exhausts you.

When you have finished the unit, you might like to come back and check the answers you have given here.

Task 1   Predicting content

Question 2 in the questionnaire asked about 'strength', 'stamina' and 'suppleness'. Can you define these three terms? What are the benefits of each?

In groups, share your ideas, and make a note of them in the 'Your ideas' column below.

	Your ideas		*Dr Davis*
		Definition	
Strength			
Stamina			
Suppleness			
		Benefits	
Strength			
Stamina			
Suppleness			

Task 2   Listening for specific information

Listen to the first part of an interview with Dr Alan Maryon Davies of The Health Education Council and check the ideas you had in your group discussion with what he says.

Put a tick in the middle column of the table if he says more or less the same as you. Put a cross if he says something different. Don't attempt to take notes yet.

Task 3   Taking notes

Listen to the interview again and, where you have put a cross in the table (i.e. where you wrote something different to what Dr Davies said), try to make a note of what Dr Davis says.

Check your notes with a partner's.

Can you now answer questions 1 and 2 in the questionnaire at the beginning of the unit?

Task 4   Sequencing information

Complete the text on each of the 'S factors' using the sentences (a–i) below.

First, decide which sentences describe which factor. Secondly, order the sentences you have selected for each factor. Have you got a coherent paragraph for each one? Make any necessary improvements to help improve the flow of the text.

True physical fitness is something more than simply being fit to cope with the stresses and strains of everyday life. It consists of three important ingredients - stamina, suppleness and strength - the S-factors.

First is *stamina* ....

Next is *suppleness* or flexibility ....

Finally, *strength* ....

---

	a	You can cope more easily with prolonged or heavy exertion, and you'll be less likely to suffer from killer heart disease.
	b	Extra muscle-power in reserve for those often unexpected heavier jobs.
	c	Toned-up tummy muscles also help to take the strain and keep your waistline trim.
1	d	This is staying power, endurance, the ability to keep going without gasping for breath.
	e	With this you have a slower, more powerful heartbeat.
	f	Lifting and shifting need strong shoulder, trunk and thigh muscles.
	g	For this you need a well-developed circulation in the heart and lungs, so that plenty of vital oxygen is pumped to your working muscles.
	h	You need to develop maximum range of movement of your neck, spine and joints to avoid straining ligaments and pulling muscles and tendons.
	i	The more mobile you are, the less likely you are to suffer aches and pains brought on by stiffness.

2 Keeping fit

Task 1   Predicting content

Before you listen to the second part of the interview with Dr Davis, read these questions and see if you can predict what his answers might be.

- What's the best way of getting and keeping fit?
- Which is better—swimming or squash? Why?
- What are the dangers of keeping fit and how can they be avoided?
- What does Dr Davis do to keep fit?

Task 2   Listening for detail

Listen to the second part of the interview to find out what answers Dr Davis actually gave to the questions.

How far were your predictions correct?

Task 3   Reading for specific information

Read the short extract below from a Health Education Council booklet and answer the following questions.

- What are the two main types of exercise?
- What is the difference between them?

> Basically, exercise is either 'static' or 'dynamic' depending on whether or not it produces movement. In static exercises (sometimes called 'isometrics'), muscles contract against resistance without any movement of the limbs.
>
> Although good for body-building, static exercises aren't much good for increasing heart and lung efficiency, which means that on their own they're *not* enough to get you fit. What's more, they can cause sudden peaks of high blood pressure - potentially harmful in the middle-aged.
>
> In dynamic exercises the limbs are moved rhythmically. The larger the muscles and the more vigorous the effort, the greater the demand for oxygen in the blood — and the better the exercise is for heart and lungs. So, for real fitness, activities involving dynamic exercise of the legs are most effective.

Which of the following activities fall into which category of exercise?

☐ cycling   ☐ walking

☐ swimming   ☐ weightlifting

☐ tug-of-war

Task 4   Classifying activities

The table below contains a list of activities. Can you give each one an S factor score?

1 = no real benefit   3 = very good effect
2 = beneficial effect   4 = excellent effect

	stamina	*suppleness*	*strength*
climbing stairs	3	1	2
cricket			
cycling (hard)			
disco dancing			
football			
golf			
gymnastics			
housework (moderate)			
jogging			
squash			
swimming (hard)			
tennis			
walking (briskly)			
weightlighting			
yoga			

- Which of these activities do you do? How beneficial are they?
- Is there anything else you do that isn't mentioned?
  How beneficial do you think it is?

Task 5   Discussion

What type of exercise would you recommend (or not recommend) for:

an unfit, overweight, middle-aged business person?
a poor student in his/her early twenties?
a housewife in her late thirties with three children under five?
a retired headteacher who's slim and fairly fit?

3 Staying young

Task 1   Listening for the main idea

Listen to part of the radio programme called 'Body Talk' in which Barbara Cartland, the romantic novelist, then aged 83, was interviewed by Michael Van Stratton.

What is Barbara Cartland's secret of keeping young?

Task 2   Listening for detail

Listen to the interview again. What does Barbara Cartland say about:

vitamins and food
her philosophy of life.

Task 3   Discussion

To what extent do Dr Davis and Barbara Cartland share the same views?

Do you agree with Barbara Cartland's two maxims for keeping fit and healthy (see her philosophy of life in Task 2)? Can you suggest alternative ones? In groups, try to agree on at least five.

Task 4   Language recap

Can you think of another word or expression that means approximately the same as the following words?

stamina
suppleness
healthy
advantage
hard (exercise)
move something heavy
hurt something

Can you think of another word or expression that means more or less the *opposite* of the following adjectives? (Try to give a context each time.)

fit
supple
powerful
gentle
beneficial
irksome
wholemeal
disagreeable

3

For everything!

1 'R' is for . . .

Task 1   Predicting content

Think back to when you were a child. What did you particularly like doing? What didn't you like doing? Tell a partner about these things and see if you had any interests in common.

What do you think parents should do to complement their children's formal education and develop their IQ?

Task 2   Listening for context

Listen to a group of 10-year-olds talking about why they do something. What are they talking about?

Compare and discuss your suggestion(s) with those of other students.

Task 3   Predicting content

Think about these two questions:

Why is it good for children to read?
What is it good for children to read?

Now make notes, according to your own opinion, in the 'You' section of the table below.

	Why is it good for children to read?
You	
The Teacher	
Differences	
	What is it good for children to read?
You	
The Teacher	
Differences	

Task 4   Listening and note taking

Now listen to Margaret Meneses, the teacher of the children you heard in Task 2, answering the two questions. Make notes in 'The teacher' section of the table, on her opinion.

Discuss your notes with a partner.

Task 5

Make a note of any differences between your opinions and those of the teacher in the 'Differences' column of the table.

Discuss these differences with a new partner.

Task 6   Discussion

Discuss the following points in groups.

- Do your present opinions on children's books reflect the reading material you had access to as a child?
- What makes a good book for children?
- What did you like reading as a child? Did you have a favourite book?
- Make a list of as many categories of children's fiction as you can think of.

2   What's it all about?

Task 1   Discussion

Look at the pictures of children's books on page 14. Which would you give to a child you know, aged between 6 and 12 years old? (A translation, if necessary.) Would you consider it from the point of view of your taste, or the child's?

Discuss your choice with a partner.

Task 2   Listening for the main idea

Listen to the same children talking about different categories of books. As they talk about each category, indicate (with numbers 1–7) which of the books represents each of the categories they are referring to.

Discuss your answers with a partner.

a

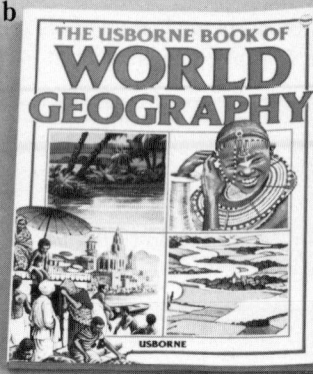

b

c

d

e

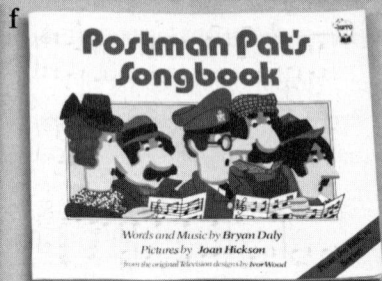

f

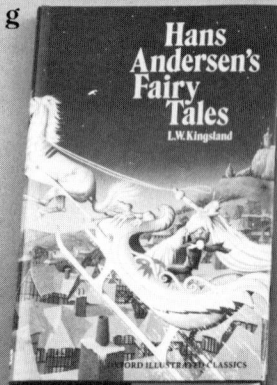

g

h

i

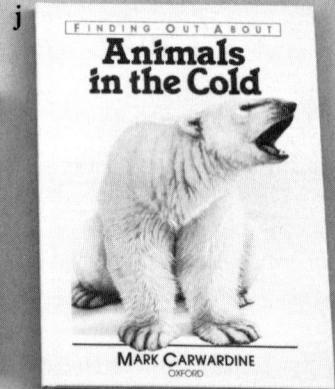

j

k

l

m

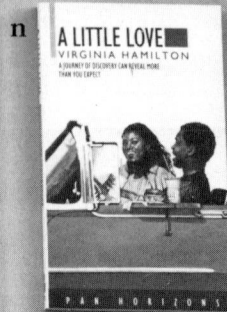

n

Task 3   Listening for keywords

Now that you have the seven books in the correct order, listen again
and write down the word or phrase you first hear which indicates the
category of book being talked about in each case.

1   ....

2   ....

3   ....

4   ....

5   ....

6   ....

7   ....

Compare your notes with those of a partner.

Task 4   Vocabulary

Look at the two lists of words below. In pairs or groups, match words
in List 1 with those in List 2 to make composite adjectives, which are
often used to describe stories, e.g. *action-packed*—used to describe
a thrilling adventure story.

List 1	*List 2*
action	fetched
fast	chilling
hard	hitting
hair	tickling
far	biting
spine	moving
nail	packed
rib	raising
tear	boggling
tongue-in	praised
highly	binding
warm	earth
down-to	jerking
thought	hearted
mind	cheek
spell	provoking

Compare your answers with those of another pair or group.

Select one of the composite adjectives which best describes a book
you have read. In your pairs or groups, each talk about the book you
have chosen and why the composite adjective describes it.

3 The storytellers

Task 1   Listening and taking notes

Listen to the interviews with two authors, Roald Dahl and Eric Carle, in which they talk about their books and what they think makes a successful children's book. As you listen make notes about the authors in the table below.

	Roald Dahl	*Eric Carle*
1 Which of his books does he mention? Which is the latest one?		
2 What does he think are the important elements in children's books?		
3 What is unusual about his books? (In terms of content or appearance)		
4 In what way is he in touch with his readers?		

Task 2   Reading and identifying the author

The extract below is from a children's book. Read it and decide,
according to what you have heard, whether it was written by Roald
Dahl or Eric Carle.

Discuss your answer with a partner and give the reason(s) for your
choice.

In the biggest brownest muddiest river in Africa, two crocodiles
lay with their heads just above the water. One of the crocodiles
was enormous. The other was not so big.

"Do you know what I would like for my lunch today?" the
Enormous Crocodile asked.

"No," the Notsobig One said. "What?"

The Enormous Crocodile grinned, showing hundreds of sharp
white teeth. "For my lunch today," he said, "I would like a
nice juicy little child."

"I never eat children," the Notsobig One said. "Only fish."

"Ho, ho, ho!" cried the Enormous Crocodile. "I'll bet if you
saw a fat juicy little child paddling in the water over there at
this very moment, you'd gulp him up in one gollop!"

"No, I wouldn't," the Notsobig One said. "Children are too
tough and chewy. They are tough and chewy and nasty and
bitter."

"*Tough* and *chewy!*" cried the Enormous Crocodile. "*Nasty*
and *bitter!* What awful tommy-rot you talk! They are juicy and
yummy!"

"They taste so bitter," the Notsobig One said, "you have to
cover them with sugar before you can eat them."

"Children are bigger than fish," said the Enormous Crocodile.
"You get bigger helpings."

Task 3   Vocabulary

In groups, look at the adjectives below and check the meanings of any you don't know.

avuncular   embittered   melancholy   mischievous   intellectual
outrageous   caring   sinister   fair   scatty   repressed
punctilious   innovative   industrious

Which of the words would you use to describe Roald Dahl or Eric Carle? Give reasons for your choice. (Listen to the interviews again if you want to.)

Roald Dahl	*Eric Carle*

Compare your choice and reasons with those of another group. What other adjectives would you add to your list for each author?

Task 4   Jigsaw listening

For this activity, the class should be divided into two groups. Each group listens to one of the four different versions of the same story. (Your teacher will decide which two versions to use.)

You are going to hear one of two children describing the same book. Each of them is re-telling the story from their own recollections and in their own way. As you listen, make notes about the story in general and any details of it that you think relevant. (You will use these notes to re-tell the story to someone who has heard a different account of it.)

Title of story	
Characters	
Relationship between characters	
Plot *Background* *Action* *Outcome*	
Unusual events	
Impressions *The child's* *Yours*	
Words you don't know (to discuss/look up later)	

Task 5   Re-telling a story

Work with a partner from the other group. Use your notes to re-tell
the story you heard to your partner. What differences and similarities
are there between the two accounts of the same story?

Which compound adjective(s) would you use to describe the story the
children were describing?

4

Genre

1 Music and images

Task 1 Building a context

Listen to the recording and try to decide:

where you would hear this music
what you think the unit is going to be about.

Task 2 Associating ideas

Listen to six short sequences of music, each of which lasts for approximately 1 minute. As you listen (without stopping the tape), write down any words that you associate with each piece of music.

1 ....

2 ....

3 ....

4 ....

5 ....

6 ....

Compare your ideas with those of a partner and then with the rest of the class.

Task 3 Discussion

Look at the photographs below and on page 21. What genre (or type) of film is each taken from?

What are the typical features of each genre? (i.e. what sort of characters, settings, etc. do they have?)

a

b

c

d

e

f

g

Task 4   Vocabulary

vampire	wagon	rifle	ghost
night club	double-cross	windscreen	saddle
court martial	revenge	gambling	tip off
neon sign	trilby	racket	cattle
ranch	surrender	sword	saloon
blackmail	stagecoach	jail	protection money

Work in small groups and decide which words above belong in which
of the sections below.

Westerns	
Gangster films	
Both genres	
Neither genre	

Task 5   Discussion

Each genre of film seems to have a limited number of themes and
story-lines. The musical, for example, is often about a group of
performers rehearsing to put on a show, and within this is a love
story: boy meets girl, boy loses girl, boy and girl get together again
(*and* become the stars of the show as well!).

What are typical themes and story-lines of westerns, melodrama and
horror films?

2 Full of men

Task 1   Listening for the main idea

Listen to the conversation between two people and try to decide what
type of film they are talking about.

What clues helped you decide?

Task 2   Listening for detail

Listen to the conversation again and make notes in the table of the
points the speakers make in favour of and against this type of film.

Check your notes with those of a partner and listen again if you want
to. (You may like to listen again with the transcript on pages 76–7 in
front of you.)

Points in favour (+)	*Points against (−)*
	full of men

Task 3   Language recap

What exactly do the speakers mean by:

a 'terribly macho . . . doing what a man's gotta do'
b 'pretty pathetic and totally unable to cope'
c 'needing the man to bail her out'
d 'the gangster's moll'
e 'they get bumped off'
f 'set up stereotypes and then undermine them'
g 'the man who identifies with the underdog'
h 'he challenges all the prevailing myths of the supremacy of the
white man'

Can you give examples from films that you have seen?

Task 4   Discussion

Are there any points made by either of the speakers that you strongly
agree or disagree with?

What do you feel about this type of film?

Do you particularly like or dislike any other genre, e.g. war films,
horror films or melodrama? Why?

5

Bulletins

1 News clues

Task 1 Predicting content

Read the eight newspaper headlines below, each of which covers a different story. In pairs, discuss what you think each story is about. Use a dictionary to help you with any unknown vocabulary.

House raiders make £15,000 jewel haul

Tragedy on way to work

Guard foiled £5,000 snatch

Hijacked plane petrol drama

Fire hits commuter train

2 hurt as gas blast wrecks flats

Drugs menace threatens world

Addict gets 3 years

Task 2 Listening for the main idea

Listen to the eight excerpts from radio news bulletins, which cover the same eight stories as the newspaper headlines. Use your predictions of the content of the stories and clues from what you hear, to match the excerpts and headlines. Write the corresponding number of each excerpt beside the corresponding headline.

Compare and discuss your answers in pairs. What words or phrases in each excerpt helped you identify the headlines?

2 Context of the news

Task 1 Listening for the main idea

📼 Listen carefully to the four stories in an excerpt from the lunch-time radio news. (Some words have been omitted from each story.) In pairs, discuss what you think each story is about.

Task 2 Listening and predicting content

📼 Listen again and write down what you think the missing words are.

a

1.................................
2.................................
3.................................
4.................................
5.................................
6.................................
7.................................
8.................................
9.................................

b

1.................................
2.................................
3.................................
4.................................
5.................................
6.................................
7.................................
8.................................

c

1.................................
2.................................
3.................................
4.................................

d

1.................................
2.................................
3.................................
4.................................
5.................................

Compare and discuss your answers in pairs. (There will often be more than one possible answer.) You may like to look at the transcript on pages 77–8 to help you with your discussion.

3 A headache for drivers

Task 1   Giving directions

In columns A and B below, are the names of different places in and around central Manchester. Work with a partner and each choose one place from each list.

Ask your partner to give you directions from Place A to Place B, using the map of central Manchester below. Imagine you are travelling by car and remember that on one-way streets you can only travel in the direction of the arrows.

Now give your partner directions between the two places that he or she has chosen. Repeat the exercise until you are familiar with the major place and street names on the map.

A	B
Victoria Station	Palace Theatre
Cathedral	Central Library
Granada TV Studios	Arndale Centre
New Century Hall	Piccadilly Station
City Exhibition Hall	BBC Studios
Salford Station	Piccadilly Gardens

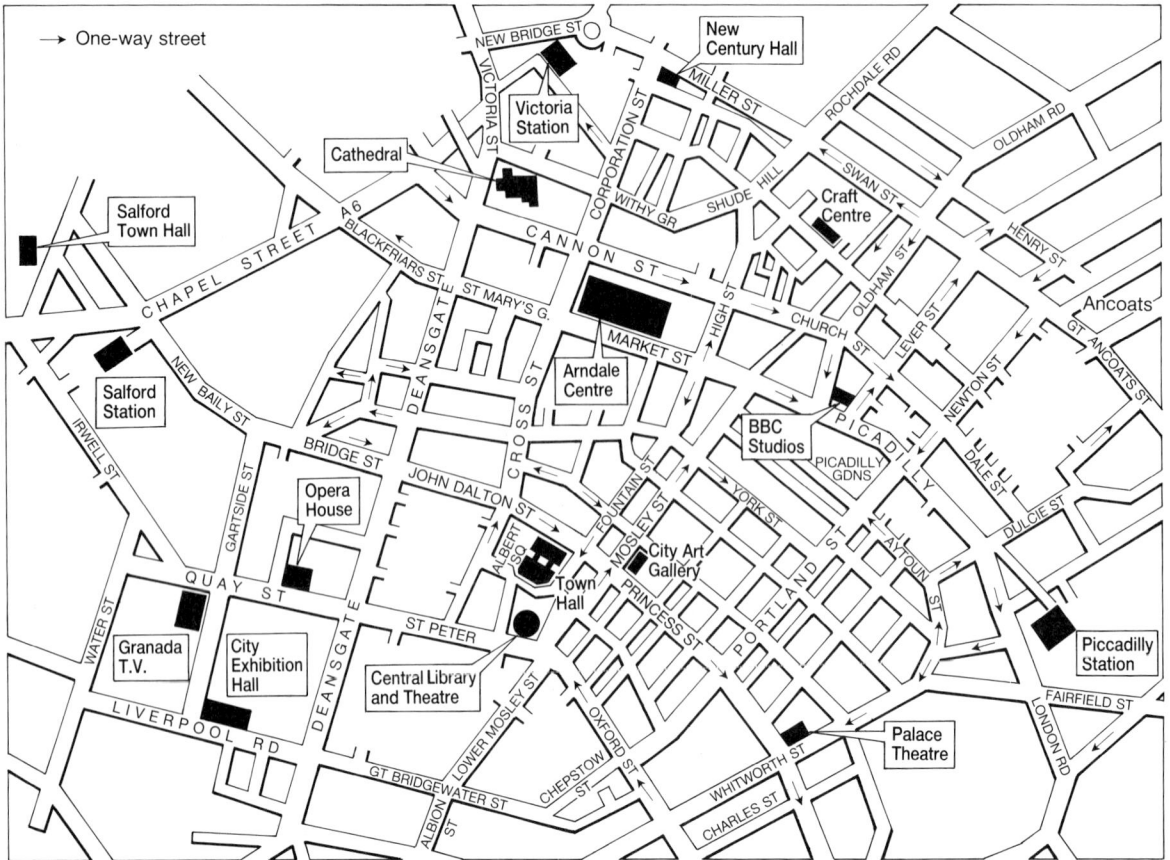

Task 2　Listening for specific information

Below are five symbols representing the reasons for different traffic delays. Listen to a bulletin of traffic information for Central Manchester and put the number of each symbol at the appropriate place on the map on page 26.

Accident

Diversion

Compare and discuss your answers in pairs or groups.

Task 3　Discussion

Now that you have the major traffic delays in central Manchester marked on your map, discuss with your partner the best route for a journey by car from Salford Town Hall to Piccadilly Station. Draw your route on the map. Try to avoid the delays and take note of the one-way street system.

Compare your route with that of another pair.

4 Tuning in

Task 1 Predicting content

Read the extract from a programme guide for five local radio stations. Try to imagine what the content of each programme will be.

Task 2 Listening for the main idea

You are now going to hear someone tuning in a radio across all five of these radio stations at a given time. You will hear short extracts from the programmes they are each broadcasting at that moment.

Listen carefully to the context clues in what you hear and identify which programmes you hear and in which order. Write the numbers 1–5 (representing the extracts) extracts against the correct programme names in the guide.

RADIO VALLEY

9.00	Parliament Report
9.25	Sportsline
9.45	Science-Fact
10.15	Wendy Rose's Shopping Guide

RADIO 207

9.00	Farmers' Diary
9.15	Financial Portfolio
9.28	The Word You Heard - Quiz programme presented by Bob de Vere
10.00	Reggae Roots

PEAK RADIO

9.00	News Round-up
9.27	Weather Word
9.30	Radio Theatre Pt. 1 *The Ordeal of Gilbert Pinfold* by Evelyn Waugh
10.00	News Round-up (with radio-car reports)

RADIO NORTH WEST

9.00	News North-West
9.10	Press Review
9.15	Family Phone-in Today's subject: Photography
10.00	Medicine Today

RIVERSIDE RADIO

9.00	Morning Service
9.10	Country Kitchen -with Dorothy Berry
9.30	Nature Trail
10.00	Riverside Notebook

Task 3 Listening for specific information

Listen to the excerpts again and decide what time of day this recording was made.

Compare your answer with that of other students.

5 Accidents will happen

Task 1   Predicting information

This section contains three bulletins, each about a transport accident. There is a report about:

a   an old aircraft which crashed on its way to an air-show
b   two ships which collided in the English Channel
c   a crash involving a passenger train and a goods train.

Below are twenty-one phrases taken from the three bulletins (seven from each). They are jumbled up. In pairs or groups, study the phrases and, before you listen to the bulletins, try to decide which of them comes from which of the news bulletins. (Some of the phrases do not obviously belong to any one story and you will have to decide about these after listening.)

Write the phrases you have selected in the appropriate column of the table on page 30.

☐	burst into flames	☐	days before the crash
☐	dental records and personal effects	☐	for information about the crash
b	he went up on deck	☐	alongside the track
☐	when their plane crashed	☐	developed engine trouble
☐	it ran into the back	☐	the Belgian vessel
☐	pronounced seaworthy	☐	there were no casualties
☐	was only slightly damaged	☐	to be taken out of service
☐	a signals failure	☐	get to the scene
☐	an official inspection	☐	was bought by
☐	off the French coast	☐	carrying fuel oil
☐	took it to air shows		

Task 2   Listening for specific information

Now listen to the three bulletins. Try to identify the phrases from Task 1 in each of them, but also pay attention to the general context and information which is given.

After listening to the bulletins, return to your pair/group-work collaboration to complete the table on page 30.

Task 3   Sequencing information

Listen to the three bulletins again. This time the twenty-one phrases from Task 1 are missing. They have been replaced by the numbers 1–7 in each bulletin.

Look at your completed table as you listen and order the phrases as they should appear in the bulletins. Use the context clues and your recollections of each report to help you.

a Air crash	b Sea collision	c Rail crash
	6 he went up on deck	

1 Symptoms and treatment

Task 1 Listening to construct a context

Listen to the extract and try to decide what it's all about. Who is talking and what is he talking about?

Task 2 Reading to construct a context

Read the text below.

... is a hormone formed in the pancreas and released into the blood stream. It promotes the uptake of glucose from the blood by the body cells; without it, glucose is neither consumed as fuel nor adequately stored, but simply accumulates in the blood until it spills over into the urine.

- What is the substance being defined?
- In what sort of book might you find such a description?
- What's the connection between this text and the recording you have just heard?

Task 3 Predicting information

Below is a list of twenty symptoms. Which ones do you think might be symptoms of the illness in question? Discuss your ideas with a partner.

☐	abdominal discomfort	☐	nausea
☐	blurred vision	☐	poor appetite
☐	dry skin	☐	recurrent boils
☐	fatigue	☐	shortness of breath
☐	headache	☐	sore, dry tongue
☐	insomnia	☐	sore throat
☐	large quantities of urine	☐	thirst
☐	loss of weight	☐	vomiting
☐	pains in the legs and feet at night	☐	wind

Do you know anything about the treatment of this illness? Discuss your ideas with the rest of the class.

6

Medicine matters

Task 4   Listening for specific information

Listen to an interview with Virginia, a nurse, and Richard who is one
of her patients.

- How did Richard first know he was ill?
- What is the role of insulin in the body? What happens in this illness?
- What is the treatment?
- Which of the symptoms listed in Task 3 does Richard mention?

Check your answers in pairs and then with the rest of the class.

Task 5   Reading for the main idea

Read the article below and try to summarize it in one or two
sentences.
Is the research it describes of use to Richard?

SCIENCE INJECTS HOPE IN DIABETES FIGHT

ROBIN McKIE
SCIENCE CORRESPONDENT

SCIENTISTS have discovered a crucial event in the sequence of biologi-
cal breakdowns that lead to diabetes.
The finding has raised the serious
prospect that people can be prevented
from developing the disorder.

Insulin injections — now used to treat
people after they have developed diabetes — would become a thing of the
past.

This new hope for diabetics follows
the discovery by British scientists of
an important factor that underpins
susceptibility to the disorder. The researchers — in Edinburgh and London — believe they may eventually be
able to pinpoint vulnerable people
and treat them before the insulin-
making parts of their pancreas are
destroyed.

New treatments are urgently needed
by doctors because cases of diabetes
are rising alarmingly in the West. In
Britain, there are now more than a
million sufferers.

'Most people do not realise it, but
diabetes is now an enormous public
health problem,' said Dr Joyce Baird,
senior lecturer at Edinburgh University's medical school.

The research — led by Dr Baird and
her collaborator, Dr Anne Cooke, of
the Middlesex Hospital medical
school, London — is the latest of a
series of recent discoveries about
diabetes, which is now known to exist
in two separate forms.

The most difficult to treat is 'insulin-
dependent diabetes' which scientists
have found is an auto-immune disease. This means the body's own
immune defences — which normally
fight off microbes and poisons — turn
on the pancreas and destroy its insulin
making cells.

The effect of this destruction is crip-
pling, because insulin is responsible
for carrying nutrition in the blood-
stream. Without it, people suffer fa-
tigue, weight loss and thirst — the
first symptoms of diabetes.

The researchers have discoverd that a
normal and pre-diabetic pancreas
react differently to a substance called
gamma interferon. This is produced
in the body to fight infections. The in-
sulin-making cells of the pre-diabetic
group, but not the other one, become
covered in chemicals called 'Class 2
HLA markers.' In turn, these markers
go on to play a crucial role in directing
the course of the disease.

'Knowing that these markers are in-
volved, we now have a variety of
strategies we can test. For example,
we could block the production of
gamma interferon, perhaps by using
antibodies that interfere with the action of gamma interferon-making
cells,' said Dr Baird.

However, the team is also working to
find out why cells become susceptible
in the first place. 'I am sure it will turn
out to be a combination of inherited
and environmental factors,' added Dr
Cooke.

Once that pathway has been worked
out, scientists may be able to develop
several different drugs that could
block the auto-immune attack. 'That
may still take a few years, but we are
very confident,' she said.

2 Holistic medicine

Task 1   Building a context

What, if anything, do you understand by a 'holistic approach' to medicine? (The short extract below may help you.)

What exactly is the writer saying? Discuss your ideas with a partner and then write one sentence to summarize the extract.

If you get spots on your tonsils, the answer is simple. Cut out your tonsils. It does not stop the bugs coming in, but they certainly can't land on your tonsils any more. This materialist conception has no room for the idea of mind or consciouness. Brain, sure, you can see that and measure it. But mind, imagination, *soul*. Oh dear, oh dear.

Alternative medicine Robert Eagle

Task 2   Listening for specific information

Listen to Vivienne, a student, talking about the differences between holistic and conventional approaches to medicine. Note down the key information about each type of medicine.

Holistic	*Conventional*

Compare your notes with those of a partner and then write one or two sentences explaining the main difference between holistic and conventional approaches to medicine.

Task 3   Vocabulary

'. . . a cardiologist . . . looks at the heart . . .'

Fill in the missing words in the table on page 34 and check your ideas with those of a partner.

Specialist	*Part of body*
cardiologist	heart
orthopaedic surgeon	
	mind
ophthalmologist	
	brain
	skin

Task 4   Discussion

Discuss the following questions in small groups.

- What do you know about acupuncture? Which part of the body does it treat?
- How does acupuncture fit in with the ideas of this section?

Task 5   Listening for specific information

Listen to the second part of the interview with Vivienne to find answers to the following questions.

- How does acupuncture work?
- What relationship did the Chinese traditionally have with their doctors?
- How does the doctor-patient relationship in the West differ from the traditional Chinese one?

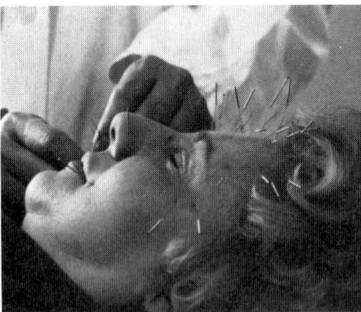

Task 6   Discussion

What is your reaction to the attitude of the Chinese to illness?

What are the qualities that *you* welcome in a doctor? In groups, decide on five important qualities from the list below and/or adding ideas of your own.

patience	a sense of humour	ability to put people at ease
sympathy	medical expertise	kindness
gentleness	a holistic approach	concern
flexibility	ability to listen	thoroughness
calmness	ability to explain	integrity
directness	a relaxed manner	ability to reassure
understanding	selflessness	willingness to spend time

1 Shattering the myth

Task 1 True or false?

7

Diamond demand

	T	F
1 There are more diamonds in the USA than		
cars	☐	☐
TV sets	☐	☐
families with children	☐	☐
dishwashers.	☐	☐
2 Diamonds are expensive because		
they are rare	☐	☐
they are controlled by a monopoly	☐	☐
they are a sort of marriage licence	☐	☐
they are difficult to mine.	☐	☐
3 Diamonds come from		
Japan	☐	☐
Israel	☐	☐
South Africa	☐	☐
Russia.	☐	☐
4 De Beers Corporation is		
an advertising agency	☐	☐
a diamond buyer	☐	☐
a diamond cutter	☐	☐
a diamond distributor.	☐	☐
5 A diamond is		
a good investment	☐	☐
forever	☐	☐
an international symbol of marriage	☐	☐
not meant to be resold.	☐	☐

When you have finished the unit, come back and check the answers you have given here.

Task 2   Predicting content

Work in pairs or in groups and look at the words and phrases below. Use a dictionary to help you with any unknown vocabulary. Try to construct a story based on these words and phrases. It should concern the set-up and workings of the international diamond industry.

diamonds --- expensive --- rare --- marriage

South African country --- best offer --- buy up --- redistribute --- monopoly

suppliers --- unlikely allies --- purely a business relationship

important economic force --- many ironies --- political power --- concealed and secretive

no real, intrinsic value --- advertising and trickery

Task 3   Listening for the main idea

Listen to the interview with Edward J. Epstein in which you will hear about the set up and workings of the international diamond business. How does Epstein's story compare with the predictions you have just made?

Compare and discuss the similarities and differences between your predictions and the account on the tape. Can you now retell the basic details of Epstein's 'story' using the words and phrases from Task 1?

Task 4   Listening for detail

Listen to the first part of the interview again and finish labelling the diagram below to show:

the role of different countries in the diamond trade
the different stages in the diamond trade.

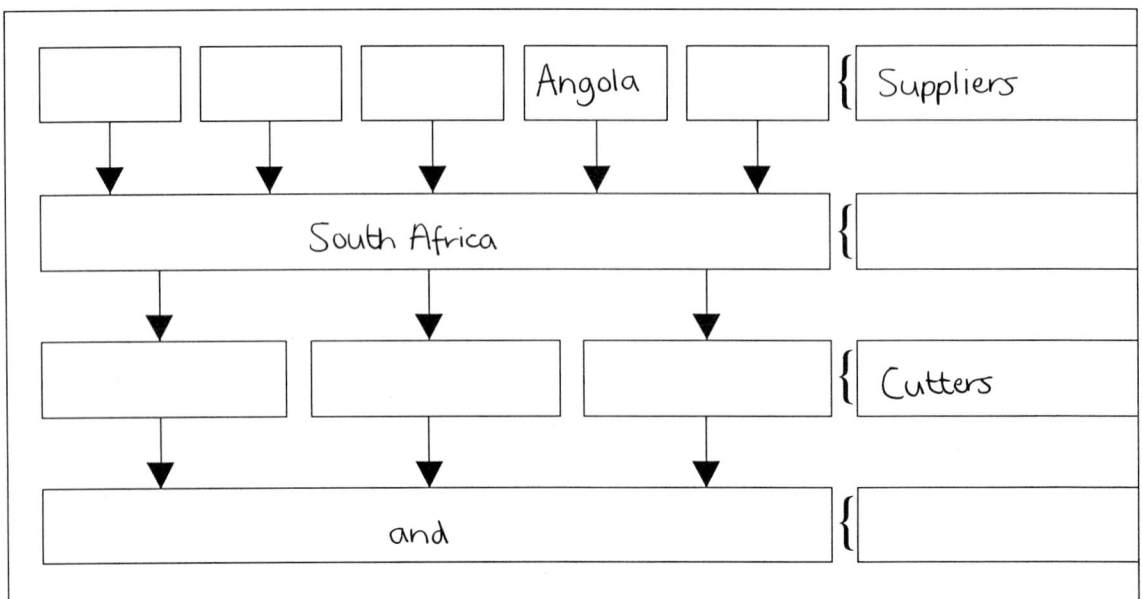

Task 5 Vocabulary

Below is a summary of the account you have already listened to. Each gap in the summary can be filled by a word or phrase, either from Task 2 or from the diagram in Task 4. Check back over these words and phrases and then work with a partner to complete the summary.

The world diamond business is largely a (1) .... controlled by a (2) .... Apart from (3) .... itself, the major (4) .... include (5) ...., (6) ...., (7) .... and (8) .... The (2) .... is able to make the (9) .... to (10) .... the diamonds from these (4) .... and so it is purely a (11) .... that brings together these (12) .... After (13) .... the rough diamonds, the (2) .... controls the supply to the market by (14) .... them. (15) .... of the diamonds subsequently takes place as they are sent to experts in (16) ...., (17) .... and (18) .... for (19) .... After the (20) .... and a clever (21) .... campaign, again controlled by the (2) .... these stones, which have (22) ...., become (23) .... gems to act as symbols of wealth and love for their (24) .... in places such as (25) .... and (26) ....

2 Creating demand

Task 1 Creating an image

You have heard how the South African De Beers Corporation controls most of the world diamond business, including the image-making advertising campaigns necessary to stimulate demand for diamonds. Imagine a country where diamonds have previously had no symbolic importance or tradition. Work with a partner or in groups and briefly discuss what images and ideas you would focus on in a campaign to open up this new market for diamonds. Can you coin any phrase or slogan, in English, which would characterize the campaign?

Compare and discuss your ideas with those of other students.

Task 2 Listening and note-taking

Listen to Epstein's account of De Beers' campaign to open up the potentially lucrative Japanese market for diamonds. As you listen, make notes, in the table on page 38, in answer to the questions on the left.

	America	Japan
1 *What is De Beers' great problem?*		
2 *Why were De Beers able to create demand?*		
3 *How did they undertake this?*	——	
4 *When did exploitation of the market take place?*		
5 *How can the short-term success of the campaign be measured?*	——	
6 *What proof is there of the lasting success of the campaign?*	——	

Task 3   Listening for detail

Listen to the second part of the interview again and write down the phrases Epstein uses which, in his account, mean the same as the phrases on page 39.

	Epstein says
a limited number of people	
a market that occurred naturally	
the greatest desire of the Japanese	
following this reasoning	
a key to becoming a westerner	
they encountered great support in Japan	
from almost nothing	

Compare and discuss your answers with a partner, or in groups.

- What are the differences between the words on the left and those on the right?
- Could these words and phrases, on the left and right, always be interchangeable?

Task 4   Discussion

You have now heard what the main idea and image behind De Beers' initial advertising in Japan was. Work with a partner and discuss what you think a typical advertisement for their campaign would look like. Try sketching your ideas on paper and add suitable slogans.

3 Diamonds are for ever

Task 1   Predicting content

Have you ever heard or seen the famous De Beers' slogan, 'A diamond is for ever'? What do you think this slogan means?

Task 2   Listening for the main idea

▣ Listen to the next part of the interview with Edward Epstein in which he discusses the slogan. Which of these four sentences best summarizes what he says?

☐ **a** Those who buy diamonds as an investment are attracted by the high profit margin which their sentimental value creates.

☐ **b** The world second-hand market for diamonds is very small because people are sentimentally attached to their diamonds and, also, De Beers has to ensure that it keeps selling new stones to maintain production levels.

☐ **c** If you think of a diamond as being 'for ever', the crucial part of it, for De Beers, is that you are going to keep it for ever.

☐ **d** A diamond is only 'for ever' if you identify it, as De Beers have done, as a symbol of everlasting love.

Compare your answer with that of other students.

Task 3   Checking information

Now check your answers to the True/False questions at the beginning of the unit. Does what you have heard make you change your mind about any of the original answers?

Task 4   Writing

Read the publicity leaflet from the London Diamond Centre, on page 41. Now that you have heard what Edward Epstein has said about the myths and realities of the diamond business, write one of the following letters:

• Write to the London Diamond Centre complaining about how you think they are misleading the public.

• You are the President of the London Diamond Centre. Write to Edward Epstein complaining about how you think he is misleading the public and, potentially, damaging your business.

What you will gain.

Apart from a unique opportunity to purchase a stone of your choice and have it set in a ring of your choice by our resident goldsmith, you can expect to gain much more from your visit.

* Appraisal - Your jewellery might be worth more than you think. Expert valuation at minimal charge from the only legally sworn appraisers in London will determine its true value and you will be offered generous trade-in prices.

* Free Advice - Diamonds may be cheaper than you think and you will be advised on a purchase which suits your pocket.

* Knowledge - Once you have been taught to determine the true worth of a diamond, you can make an informed purchase anywhere in the world.

* The best advice in London - The Chairman and President of The London Diamond Centre are acknowledged international experts and the greatest diamond authorities in London.

* Entertainment - The permanent exhibition is a completely fascinating experience well worth a visit.

What you will see.

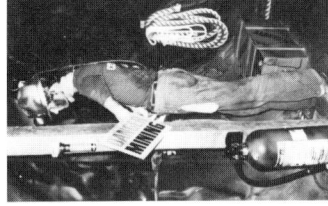

At the London Diamond Centre you will see an exhibition which shows a diamond from its mining, through cutting, sawing and shaping to the final faceting and polishing.

You can see the gem being mounted and set in a ring by the resident goldsmith and the magnificent collection of diamonds, stones and jewellery displayed in elegant showcases.

If you wish, you can receive expert guidance in appraising diamonds and assessing their true worth - an invaluable piece of knowledge.

The London Diamond Centre is unique.

The London Diamond Centre offers so much more than a jewellery shop. Not only does it have the largest collection of diamonds, precious and semi-precious stones to be found anywhere in London, but it also offers visitors the chance to see how diamonds are transformed from rough stones into glittering gems, and to purchase jewellery tax-free, at factory prices.

Opening hours:
9.30 to 5.30 Monday to Friday
9.30 to 1.30 Saturday

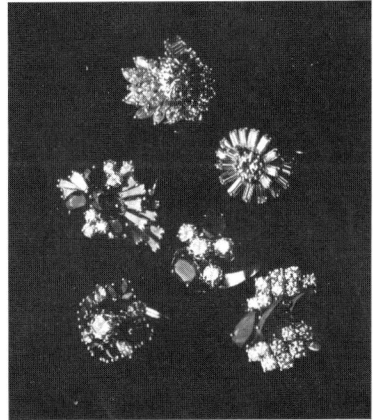

8

Flying around freely

1 A special kind of farm

Task 1 Building a context

📼 Listen to the extract and try to decide:

what is being talked about
who is doing the talking.

Task 2 Vocabulary

What words do you already know relating to butterflies?
Try to label the drawings below. If you have any problems, try
making a guess and then check it in a dictionary or with your teacher.

1 ....

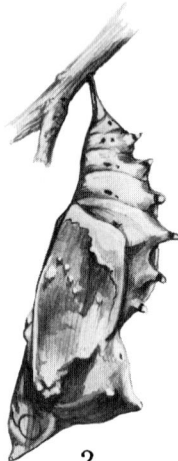

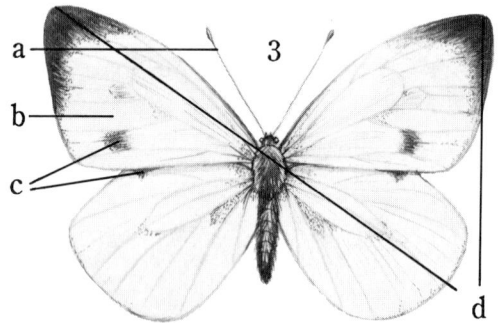

2 ....   e ....

Task 3 Reading for specific information

Have you ever heard of a butterfly farm? What is it (or what do you
think it might be)? Discuss your ideas briefly with the rest of the
class.

Work in groups of three. Each of you should read a different one of
the three texts below to find out what you can expect to see in a
butterfly farm, then tell the other two the gist of what you have read.

A Here the air is usually alive with the colourful vibrant wings of exotic
butterflies of every shape and hue. By careful planning and control, a
tropical environment has been created which favours the healthy
progression of the butterflies through every stage of their life cycle. By
virtue of the protection provided them from their natural enemies, visitors
to the Butterfly Farm are in the unique position of being able to walk
amongst these enchanting creatures and observe them as they carry out
their daily routines in an unselfconscious manner.

B A butterfly farm is a place where we collect exotic butterflies by buying them in from all parts of the world, in the chrysalis stage by the way, not actually buying adult butterflies, and they are allowed to hatch and release into a tropical environment which is very realistic to what you might see somewhere in South America or the Far East, where they can fly about and live freely and people can experience them—this is the paying public—can come in and experience them flying around freely as they would in the wild.

C Rain or shine, explore the tropical jungle paradise where the air is heavy with the perfume of nectar-rich flowers. Wander among hundreds of free-flying butterflies from all over the world. Closely observe and photograph all stages of breeding, egg-laying, caterpillar rearing and courtship displays. See our tropical pool planted with giant water lilies, listen to the sound of jungle streams and bubbling rock springs. Separate gallery containing other fascinating insects such as giant spiders, scorpions, stick insects and locusts. Pictorial and educational displays.

Now discuss these questions in your group.
- Which text tells you the most? Why do you think this is?
- Where would you expect to find each text?
- Would you expect to read it or hear it? What clues helped you decide?
- Can you find anything ambiguous in the wording of Text A?

Task 4 Predicting content

Before you listen to the interview with Barrie Jolliffe, entomologist and manager of the Weymouth Butterfly Farm, read the questions below and think about possible answers to them.
- How big is the farm and what does it consist of?
- What does it feel like to be inside a butterfly farm?
- What sort of plants are used and why?
- What's the purpose of the farm?
- In what ways is it novel?

Compare your ideas with those of other students.

Task 5 Listening for specific information

Listen to the interview to find out the answers to the questions above. Make notes if you want to.

When you have finished, compare your answers and notes with those of another student. How close were your ideas in Task 4 to the 'real' answers?

The transcript of this text is on page 82. You may like to listen to the interview again with the transcript in front of you.

2 Family life

How much do you know about butterflies?

1 How many families of butterfly are there altogether in the world?
 a 15   **c** 500
 b 150   **d** 5000.

2 The largest butterflies are about:
 a 10 inches   **c** 14 inches
 b 12 inches   **d** 16 inches.

3 Which of the following is a type of butterfly?
 a village green   **c** cabbage white
 b navy blue   **d** garden violet.

4 Bright red or orange markings on a butterfly may signify:
 a an invitation—'Come and get me.'
 b a warning—'Don't eat me.'
 c a threat—'I'll bite you.'
 d nothing—they're purely decorative.

5 Which butterflies can stay out in the sun longest?
 a black ones   **c** red ones
 b yellow ones   **d** blue ones.
 Why?

6 Some butterflies . . .
 a are poisonous   **c** travel thousands of miles
 b produce static electricity **d** don't like sunshine.

When you have finished this unit, you might like to come back and check the answers you have given here.

Note: Some questions have more than one correct answer.

Task 1   Jigsaw listening—for key words

For this activity, the class should be divided in half. Each half listens to a different half of the interview.

You are going to hear Barrie Jolliffe talking about various butterflies and butterfly families. In all he describes eight families, but you will hear information about only four of them.

As you listen, look at the pictures on page 45 and choose the picture which illustrates the butterfly or family Barrie is describing. Write the letter of the picture in the first column of the table on page 46.

Check your suggestions with other people in the group to make sure you agree.

Task 2   Jigsaw listening—for specific information

📧 Listen to Barrie again and take notes under the headings given in the
table on page 46. (Note: Not all the information is given for every
family.)

Check your notes with those of another student. Listen again if
necessary (stop and replay bits if you need to).

Task 3   Listening with the transcript

The transcript of this recording is on pages 83–84. You may like to check your notes against it — especially for the spelling of some of the words.

Listen to the extract again and read it to yourself at the same time: this will help fix the pronunciation of some of the new items and the stress and rhythm of connected speech.

Picture letter	Family	Butterfly common name	Colours	Food	Distri-bution	Habitat	Special notes
	Brassolidae						
	Danidae						
	Heliconidae						
	Papilionidae						
	Pieridae						
	Lycaenidae						
	Morphidae						
	Nymphalidae						

Task 4   Finding out more

Work with a partner from the other group to find out about and make notes on the four butterfly families for which you have no information.

Task 5   Discussion

- What sorts of butterflies are most common in your country?
- What do they look like?
- What else do you know about them? (Use the table above to help you.)

Task 6   Writing

Choose two of the families described by Barrie Jolliffe and write a short descriptive paragraph on each, using the notes in your table.

3 Conservation

Task 1   Predicting content

At the end of the interview, the interviewer asks Barrie Jolliffe two final questions:

'Can you say something about the problems that butterflies are having in the countryside today? What's happening in the countryside and why are butterflies becoming scarcer?'

'And what can ordinary people do to try and help butterflies?'

Can you predict what his answers might be?

Task 2   Listening for the main ideas

Listen to the extract to see how far your ideas coincide with Barrie's.

Task 3   Discussion

Here is a slogan from a BBCS (British Butterfly Conservation Society) poster with some of the words removed.

Can you replace the missing words and also think of another 'punchy' slogan for their "Save the Butterfly" campaign.

You can help to save British Butterflies. Join the BBCS. Plant your garden with ....

Create and maintain truly wild areas of habitat. Report to us any .... to habitats. Control the use of .... and ....

.... to the Society's Reserve Fund for the management and purchase of butterfly reserves

9

Egypt for the day

1 An eventful day

Task 1 Discussion

This unit is about a group of tourists on a rather exclusive tour. They leave London one Saturday morning for a day out in Cairo and are back in Britain, in time for bed, the same day.

In groups, discuss how you think the tourists manage this unusual journey, what they see and do during the day and why anyone would want to go on such a trip. Would you?

Task 2 Sequencing events

Below is a list of the different stages in this incredible day out. Listen to eleven extracts from the day's events. Match the number of each extract to the stage of the day you think it concerns. The first one has been done for you.

	before leaving London
	leaving London
	an early stage of the journey
1	a meal en route
	approaching Cairo
	arrival in Cairo
	a drive through the city
	a guided sightseeing tour
	after the tour
	the return journey
	arrival in London

Compare your answers in pairs or groups and listen again, if necessary, to check your answers.

Task 3 Identifying specific words and phrases.

Read the phrases below, checking any vocabulary, if necessary. One phrase in each group is the same as in the corresponding extract on the recording. Listen to the extracts again and tick the phrases you hear.

1 a We eat an early lunch and drink some champagne.

b We ate an early lunch and drank some champagne.

c We eat an early lunch then drink some more champagne.

2 a We struggle past the armed soldiers.

   b We straddle past the armed soldiers.

   c We straggle past the armed soldiers.

3 a We're started drinking.

   b We started drinking.

   c We'd started drinking.

4 a 100,000 men

   b 10,000 men

   c 1,000 men

5 a already they'd taken

   b already they were taking

   c already they're taking

6 a I'll see the camel

   b I'd seen the camel

   c I've seen the camel

7 a and then we'll be back once more

   b and then we are back once more

   c and then we were back once more

8 a We seem to be airborne

   b We seemed to be airborne

   c We'd seemed to be airborne

9 a you'll have a very, very pleasant day

   b you've had a very, very pleasant day

   c you had a very, very pleasant day

10 a we'll be starting to slow up

   b we'd be starting to slow up

   c we'd been starting to slow up

11 a watching as silently as we glide by

   b watching as, silently, we glide by

   c watching us silently as we glide by

Task 4   Discussion

From what you have heard so far, how correct were you in the
predictions you made, before listening, about the content of this day
out?

2 Day trippers

Task 1   Vocabulary

Work in pairs or groups and look at the words or phrases below. Use
a dictionary to check any unknown vocabulary.

just saved up   rickety lorries   lump sum   overwhelming
a bother   indulgence   barmy   worthwhile   windscreen wipers
your ears start to pop   looking as if they're going to throw up
all expecting big tips   rather scared   to kneel down   one heck of a lot
has put me quite at ease   one-upmanship   staggeringly rich
flashy people   lop-sided

Task 2   Identifying words and phrases

Listen to interviews with six of the passengers on the trip and, after
each interview, underline any of the vocabulary and phrases above,
which you hear.

Check your answers in pairs or groups and listen again, if necessary.

Task 3   Recalling information

In groups, try to fill in some of the table below with any information
that you can remember from the interviews in Task 2.

Task 4   Listening and taking notes

Listen to the six interviews again and make notes in the table. (Note:
Not all the questions can be answered for each passenger.)

Compare and discuss your answers in pairs or groups and listen again
for confirmation.

	What are their reasons for being on the trip?	How do they consider themselves?	What do their friends at home think?	What are their impressions of the trip?
Elderly woman from the south of England		–		
Young woman from the south of England		–		
Middle-aged man from the north-east of England		–		
Middle-aged man from the south of England		–		
Young man from the south-west of England	–		–	
Late middle-aged woman from the north-west of England			–	

3 Your captain speaking

Task 1 Matching questions and answers

The next recording contains extracts from an interview with the pilot of the aircraft. Match the pilot's answers, which are on the tape, with the interviewer's questions on page 52. Write the number of each answer in the box beside the question which you think produced it. (Note: the answers on the tape are not necessarily in the same order as the questions.)

a 'Where are we at the moment?' ☐

b 'How high are we at the moment?' ☐

c 'So we are still climbing?' ☐

d 'Do you ever get used to flying this aircraft? Is it always something a bit more special than just the kind of average aircraft you might fly? ☐

e 'You're very generous in allowing passengers to come up and look at the flight-deck. Is that really a bother, or is that something you enjoy?' **1**

f 'And how do you get to fly a Concorde? Have you had a long career in other sorts of aircraft and now you've graduated to this?' ☐

g 'How much does the plane really fly itself and how much are you having to monitor a lot of things all the time?' ☐

h 'One of the signs I didn't expect to see was a little label over there, I can see, that says , "Do not open window in flight". Is that really necessary to have that label there?' ☐

i 'What would happen if you could open that window? What would happen to us now if that window were open?' ☐

j 'Finally, when we started to talk we were just coming up to Crete. We seem to be making a turn, now. Where are we now?' ☐

Compare and discuss your answers in pairs or groups.

Task 2   Recalling information

In your groups, look at the interviewer's questions again and try to remember any details of the pilot's answers to each of them. Write down any details you agree on, leaving enough space to add more notes later.

Task 3   Listening and taking notes

Listen to the pilot's answers again and make notes, individually, to add to any you have already made.

Compare and exchange your information with other members of your group and then report what you have collectively written to the whole class. Add any further information to your individual notes.

Task 4   Recognizing stress and intonation

Look back at the interviewer's questions in Task 1 and, in pairs, read out the underlined parts of the questions with what you think should be the appropriate stress, intonation and linking of words.

▣ Now listen to a recording of the interviewer's questions. You will hear
each question twice. As you listen, mark the stressed syllables and
rises and falls in intonation on the text.
For example: 'Where are we at the moment?'
Compare and discuss your answers in pairs or groups. Listen again
and repeat the questions in the pauses.

Task 5   Role play

In pairs, improvise an interview similar to the one you have heard,
using your notes from Tasks 2 and 3 to help you. Take it in turns to be
the pilot and the interviewer.

4 From beginning to end

Task 1   Predicting content

Look at the advertisement for this day-trip below and the two maps
on page 54. Fill in any information you already know and decide what
information you need to listen for.

EGYPT

FOR THE DAY BY

_____

Only_____ seats on this exclusive,
once-in-a-lifetime trip.
The price of £ _____ includes:
* _____before departure.
* _____ on the outbound journey.
* _____ on the return journey.
* sightseeing tour of Cairo by _____
   with the services of a _____ and a
* ride by _____ or _____ or
   _____ at the site of the Pyramids
   (_____ are not included).
* a buffet lunch at the _____.
Leave London at _____ on Saturday
13th March and arrive back at _____ ,
spending _____ hours in Cairo!

Task 2   Listening for specific information

▣ Listen to the complete account of the day out to Cairo, which includes
the extracts and interviews you have already heard. As you listen,
complete the missing information on the advertisement and indicate
the route to Cairo and the places visited there, on the maps.

Compare and discuss your answers in pairs or groups.

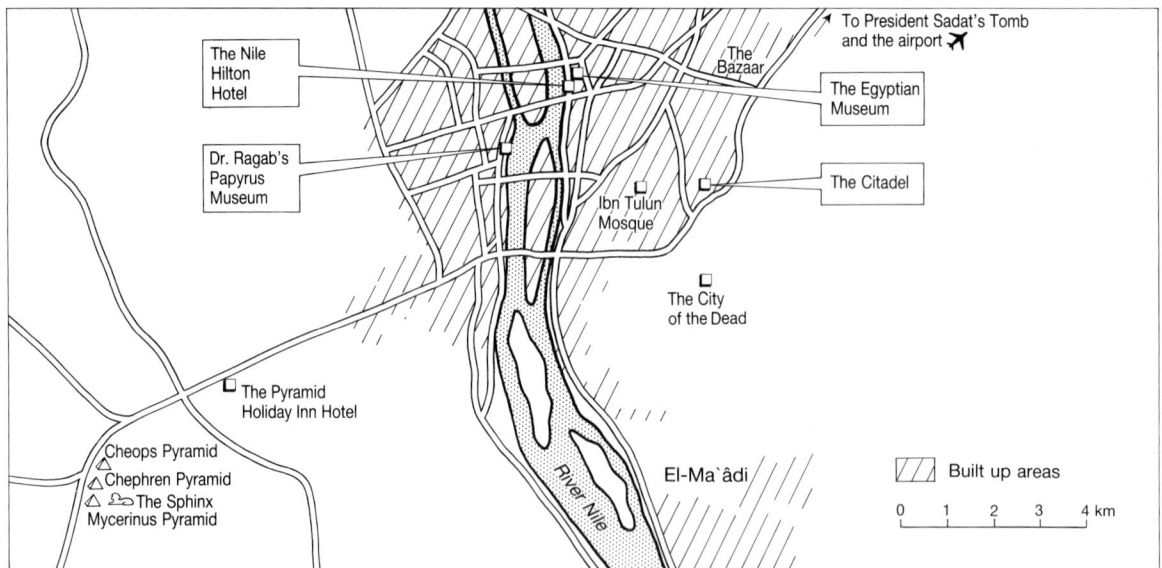

Task 3   Discussion

Imagine that you were able to go to any one place in the world for a supersonic day out.

- Where would you go? Why?

- Who would you take with you?

- What would you do there? Remember you only have a day to complete the whole trip.

Present your plans and itinerary to the other members of your group and be prepared to answer questions and discuss the relative merits of your own and other people's proposed day-trips.

1 Functions

Task 1 Predicting content

This section includes a series of extracts from speeches and public comments made by famous people. The purposes of these speeches or comments fall into the following categories:

reassurance	warning
denial	paying a tribute
promise	resignation from a post
expressing an opinion	acceptance of a post

Work in pairs or groups, and write down any phrases or structures that you would use to express these functions.

Compare your ideas with those of another pair or group.

Task 2 Recognizing functions

Now listen to the sixteen extracts and tick the columns according to which function each extract has. The first one has been done for you.

										Extract number						
Function	1	2	3	4	5	6	7	8	9	10	11	12	13	14	15	16
Reassurance																
Denial																
Promise																
Expressing an opinion																
Warning																
Paying a tribute																
Resignation from a post																
Acceptance of a post																

Alger Hiss

John Paul II

Martin Luther King Jr

Richard Nixon

Task 3   Listening for detail

Listen to the extracts again and, where possible, write down examples of the language or structures used which enabled you to identify the functions.

2 Proverbs

This section looks at some proverbs in English. Although used sparingly in everyday conversation, they tend to crop up when the speaker is stuck for something more appropriate to say. The actual meanings of these proverbs must be learnt, as they are not obvious from the individual words that make them up.

Task 1   Predicting content

The words in columns A and B of the table below can be used to make twelve English proverbs, e.g. *Silence is golden*. Do you recognise any others? Work in pairs or groups and try to predict what some of them might be.

In the 'Prediction' column, write the numbers of the words in Column A and the letters of the words in Column B that you think they go with to make a proverb. The first one has been done for you.

A	B	Prediction	Listening	Proverbs
1 silence	a hear	1c	1c	Silence is golden.
2 rains	b fire			
3 lovely weather	c golden			
4 pennies	d pours			
5 everything comes	e ducks			
6 can't believe	f spilled milk			
7 no smoke	g he who waits			
8 only get	h silver lining			
9 every cloud	i feather			
10 crying	j pay for			
11 knock down	k pounds			

Task 2 Recognizing proverbs

Listen to the radio advertisement for a car which features a conversation between two men, Dennis and Richard. It is hardly a realistic conversation as it is almost entirely made up of proverbs. How many can you identify?

Compare your answers with those of a partner and then discuss where and why the conversation took place.

Task 3 Listening for detail

Listen to the advertisement again and match the two halves of the proverbs. Write the numbers of the words in Column A and the letters of the corresponding words in Column B in the 'Listening' column.

How many of your predictions were correct?

Task 4 Discussion

In groups, write a list of the complete proverbs in the right-hand column of the table. Discuss what you think they mean and when you might use them.

Can you remember hearing any other proverbs apart from those in the table above? Listen again and then check your ideas by reading the transcript on page 91. Which of the proverbs have similar meanings?

Task 5   Identifying speaker's mood and attitude

Listen to five extracts from different conversations. After each one decide which of the proverbs from Task 4 you might respond with if that person were talking to you. Write down your answers and then compare and discuss them with a partner.

Task 6   Discussion

Do *you* use proverbs in English? Do you think you could use any (more) now? Are there any proverbs in your own language which are used in similar situations to the ones you have met in this section? What do they say?

3 Moods

Task 1   Predicting content

Look at the list of adjectives below and check that you understand them all. In pairs, discuss briefly how such features as voice-type, voice range, stress and intonation can be used to signal these moods or attitude when people speak. Give examples to illustrate your ideas.

nonchalant	amused
interested	threatening
bored	superior
excited	polite
happy	nervous
sad	pleasant
distressed	mocking
mysterious	impatient
suspicious	frightened
surprised	defiant

Task 2   Identifying speakers' mood and attitude

Listen to the compilation of four recordings: a poem, an extract from a radio play, another advertisement for a car, and a rather unusual train announcement. As you listen, tick those adjectives which you would use to describe the voices you hear.

Compare your answers in pairs or groups.

Task 3   Listening for detail

Write the adjectives you have chosen for each section of the compilation in the appropriate box below (there may be some repetition). Listen to the recording again, stopping after each section, and note down particular language or voice features which helped you in your choice of adjectives.

	Adjectives	Notes
Poem		
Play man girl	defiant	'You've got no right at all. Do you hear?' 'Réspect' (intonation)
Advertisement Voice 1 Voice 2		
Announcement		

Compare and discuss your notes in pairs or groups.

Task 4   Activating what you've learnt

In pairs, write a short dramatic presentation to be read or acted aloud
to the class. You may get some ideas by thinking about the different
types of recordings you have listened to in this unit. Try to use a
variety of the aspects of voice, vocabulary and structure that has been
covered in this unit. The choice is yours!

KEY

UNIT 1
Section 1
Task 1
Event/setting: dinner party in someone's house

People and relationships: Ted and his wife (the hosts) a
second couple (the guests)
  The guests may not be close friends of the hosts'
  because Ted refers to his wife as 'my wife' rather than
  by her name.

Topic: a cooking pot called a tajine which is presumably on
the table and which the hosts brought back from
Morocco.

Section 2
Task 1
The singer is being ironic and doesn't like dinner parties at
all. She obviously thinks they are superficial occasions on
which people say what they're expected to say—which is
often the opposite of what they're thinking.

She uses the expression 'frightfully super' as an ironic
accolade. The expression has upper-class connotations as,
traditionally, do formal dinner parties.

Task 3, 4 and 5
See page 69 for the complete transcript of the song.

Section 3
Task 4
1d small talk **2b** fun and games **3e** bored to tears
4g polite noises **5c** drop names **6i** pluck up
courage **7f** miss the mark **8a** lose face **9h** skirt
the issue.

UNIT 2
Section 1
Questionnaire
1c 2b 3a 4a

Task 4
Stamina d e g a
Suppleness h i
Strength b f c

Section 2
Task 2
getting/keeping fit: 'you . . . have to do a little bit more
each day, or even every other day for that matter.'

swimming v. squash: 'swimming is . . . particularly
excellent for all three of the S-factors.' 'squash though is
not a good way to *get* fit.'

dangers: confusing keeping fit with getting fit. 'you could
do yourself a lot of damage by playing squash if you're not
in good physical shape to start with.'

Dr Davis: does a lot of walking and cycling around London.

Task 3
static exercise: exercises muscles, but doesn't produce
any movement of the limbs, e.g. tug-of-war, weightlifting

dynamic exercise: limbs are moved rhythmically, e.g.
cycling, swimming, walking.

Task 4

	stamina	suppleness	strength
climbing stairs	3	1	2
cricket	1	2	1
cycling (hard)	4	2	3
disco dancing	3	4	1
football	3	3	3
golf	1	2	1
gymnastics	2	4	3
housework (moderate)	1	2	1
jogging	4	2	2
squash	3	3	2
swimming (hard)	4	4	4
tennis	2	3	2
walking (briskly)	2	1	1
weightlifting	1	1	4
yoga	1	4	1

Section 3
Task 1
vitamins, eating properly, thinking positively

Task 2
Avoid white bread and sugar. Eat nourishing food rather
than a lot of food. Vitamins are important because they are
pure food.

'You are what you eat.'
'You become what you think.'

Task 4
synonyms
stamina: endurance, staying power
suppleness: flexibility, mobility
healthy: fit
advantage: benefit
hard (exercise): demanding, vigorous, arduous, energetic
move something heavy: shift
hurt something: damage

opposites
fit: unfit
supple: stiff
powerful: weak
beneficial: detrimental, damaging

irksome: enjoyable, fun
wholemeal: refined
disagreeable: nice, cheerful, friendly

UNIT 3

Section 1

Task 2

The children are talking about why they enjoy reading

Task 4

Why is it good for children to read?

The teacher: to expand their vocabulary and help them to
do better in other subjects
keeps them from doing things they shouldn't be doing!
improves their language and expands their experiences
of what happens in the world
gives them independence, e.g. ability to read
instructions, etc.

What is it good for children to read?

The teacher: everything – mystery books, science fiction,
newspapers, magazines, signs, textbooks, comics, back
of cereal packet.

Section 2

Task 3

1 n 'kiss'
2 h 'rhymes'
3 c 'flowers'
4 a 'haunted'
5 j 'animals'
6 d 'rhyming ones and unrhyming ones'
7 m 'exciting, adventure, robbery, kidnapping'

Task 4

action-packed fast-moving hard-hitting hair-raising
far-fetched spine-chilling nail-biting rib-tickling
tear-jerking tongue-in-cheek highly-praised warm-
hearted down-to-earth thought-provoking mind-
boggling spell-binding

Section 3

Task 1

Roald Dahl

1 *The BFG*
Charlie and the Chocolate Factory
Danny the Champion of the World
James the Giant Peach
The Witches (latest)
2 magic
spookiness
fun/laughter
strong plot (plausible)
3 content – ordinary people
are witches, etc.
daring – 'whiz-popping'
4 children write to him
spends 1 hour per day
reading their letters

Eric Carle

1 *The Very Hungry Caterpillar*
The Mixed-up Chameleon
The Very Busy Spider (latest)
2 half toy/half book
outrageous, nonsensical
humour (not subtle)
children learn things, e.g. telling time, days of the
week, colours, counting, i.e. combine teaching with
fun/storyline
3 always about small animals
contain holes/folds and, e.g.
touchable spider's web, fly & spider
4 In sympathy with insecurity of childhood
'It's tough to be small . . .' (relates to own childhood)
Visits schools and involves children in the book-making
process, e.g. *The Mixed-up Chameleon*

Task 2

The extract is taken from *The Enormous Crocodile* by
Roald Dahl

Task 3

Suggested answers (v = impression derived from voice,
c = impression derived from context)

Roald Dahl: avuncular (v) sinister (v) mischievous (c)
caring (c) industrious (c)

Eric Carle: melancholy (v) scatty (v) innovative (c) fair (c)
caring (c) punctilious (c)
(NB 'outrageous' is his word to describe the humour
needed for children's books)

Task 5

far-fetched, mind boggling

UNIT 4

Section 1

Task 1

The music is the sort which would be played as an
accompaniment to a silent film, i.e. one made without a
soundtrack, before the days of 'talkies'. It would therefore
be heard in a cinema.

Task 2

The pieces of music are (in order) extracts from
soundtracks of a James Bond (spy) film, a melodrama (love
story), a western, a comedy, a thriller and a war film.

Task 3

a war film b horror film c western d crime film
e gangster film f musical g comedy

Task 4

Westerns court martial ranch wagon stagecoach rifle
saddle cattle saloon
Gangster films night club neon sign trilby windscreen
racket protection money
both double-cross revenge surrender gambling
jail tip-off blackmail
neither vampire sword ghost

Section 2

Task 2

Points in favour

some work against the genre, undermine stereotypes, e.g. identify with the underdog (Indians)

portray lonely hero who is against society – self sufficient, competent man who challenges the myth of white supremacy

humorous, one-off lines

Points against

full of men

very few women characters

men very macho

women portrayed as pathetic or threatening (in which case, killed off)

violent

portrayal of the Indians

UNIT 5

Section 1

Task 2

Excerpt no.	Headline
1	'Hijacked plane petrol drama'
2	'Fire hits commuter train'
3	'Drugs menace threatens world'
4	'House raiders make £15,000 jewel haul'
5	'2 hurt as gas blast wrecks flats'
6	'Tragedy on way to work'
7	'Addict gets 3 years'
8	'Guard foiled £5000 snatch'

Section 2

Task 2

a 1 airports
   2 delayed
   3 destinations
   4 flights
   5 aircraft
   6 patience
   7 travelling
   8 airlines
   9 protesting

b 1 figures
   2 drop/decrease/reduction
   3 students
   4 rise/increase
   5 paint/show/present
   6 fall/decrease/reduction
   7 steps/action
   8 economy

c 1 robbers/raiders
   2 jewellery
   3 open
   4 getaway/escape

d 1 died
   2 accident
   3 lorry
   4 injuries
   5 witnesses

Section 3

Task 2

Symbol 3 (accident) on Chapel Street, A6, between Bridge Street and Blackfriars Street.

Symbol 1 (fire) on John Dalton Street at junction with Cross Street and Albert Square

Symbol 4 (burst water main) on Cannon Street, between Deansgate and Corporation Street.

Symbol 5 (diversion) on Great Ancoats Street, parallel with Henry Street, between Ancoats and Oldham Road.

Symbol 2 (roadworks) on Mosley Street, between Princess Street and Piccadilly Gardens.

Section 4

Task 2

1 'Family phone-in' (photography) Radio North-West
2 'The Word you Heard' (quiz programme) Radio 207
3 'Country Kitchen' Riverside Radio
4 'Weather Word' Peak Radio
5 'Sportsline' Radio Valley.

Task 3

Time of recording: 9.29 a.m.

Section 5

Tasks 1 and 3

	Air crash		*Sea collision*		*Rail crash*
6	dental records and personal effects	6	he went up on deck	2	burst into flames.
1	when their plane crashed	3	pronounced seaworthy	5	it ran into the back
2	an official inspection	2	was only slightly damaged	6	a signals failure
4	took it to air-shows	1	off the French coast	7	for information about the crash
7	days before the crash	5	the Belgian vessel	3	alongside the track
5	developed engine trouble	7	there were no casualties	4	get to the scene
3	was bought by	4	be taken out of service	1	carrying fuel oil

---

UNIT 6

Section 1

Task 1

A diabetic patient is talking about a new method of injecting himself with insulin.

Task 2
Insulin

The description comes from the Penguin Medical Encyclopaedia.

The text describes insulin which is used in the treatment of diabetes and is normally injected using a syringe. (This is what the speaker in Task 1 is describing.)

Task 3
The following are symptoms of diabetes:

thirst, large quantities of urine, loss of weight, constipation, recurrent boils, dry skin, sore dry tongue, leg and foot pains at night, blurred vision.

Task 4
The symptoms mentioned by Richard are thirst, sweating a lot, feeling lethargic and large quantities of urine.

Task 5
It is possible that certain people are susceptible ('genetically predisposed') to certain diseases, one of which is diabetes. Using a substance called gamma inteferon, which causes a different reaction on a normal and on a pre-diabetic pancreas, it may be possible to pinpoint these people in the future, and so prevent them from getting the disease.

This research is too late to help Richard because he already has the disease, and it is quite advanced.

Section 2
Task 1
Because the mind is intangible and cannot be measured, it cannot be recognized as a factor in illness. The writer is against this type of thinking that dismisses the role of the mind in illness.

Task 2
Holistic
Considers the whole person – physical, emotional, spiritual and the *whole* body, not just individual parts.
Conventional
Produces people who specialize in one part of the body, e.g. cardiologist specializes in the heart. Doesn't relate the problem part to the rest of the body.

Task 3
cardiologist	heart
orthopaedic surgeon	bones
ophthalmologist	eyes
neurologist	brain
dermatologist	skin

Task 6
Acupuncture restores imbalances within the body's energy system.

Traditionally Chinese visited their doctor several times a year and only paid him/her when they were kept well. If they became ill, they didn't pay.
In the west, doctors (including those practising acupuncture) are not using preventative medicine.
Patients ignore symptoms of illness until they become very ill (are 'carted off in an ambulance').

UNIT 7
Section 1
Task 1
1 T, F, T, T
2 F, T, F, F
3 F, F, T, T
4 F, T, F, T
5 F, F, T, T

Task 4

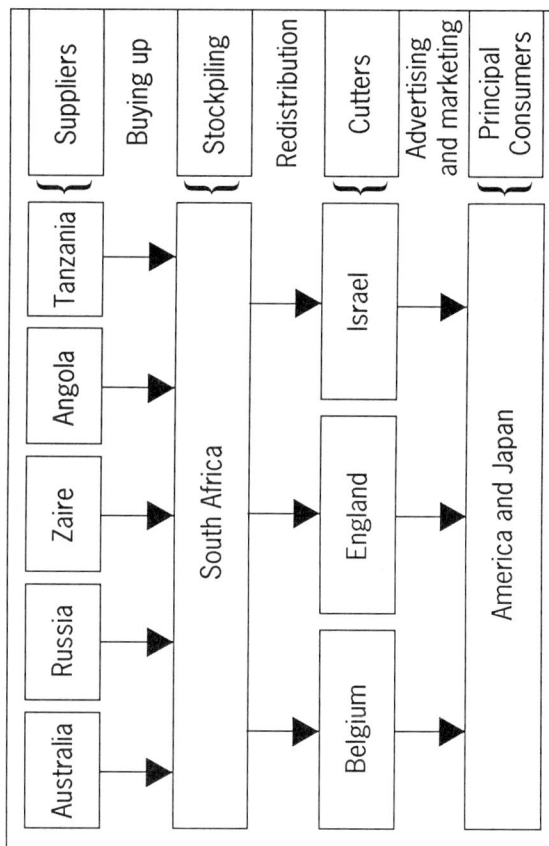

Task 5
1 monopoly
2 South African company
3 South Africa
4 suppliers
5 Zaire ⎤
6 Angola ⎟ any order
7 Tanzania ⎟
8 Russia ⎦
9 best offer
10 buy up
11 business relationship
12 unlikely allies
13 buying up
14 stockpiling
15 distribution
16 Belgium ⎤
17 England ⎬ any order
18 Israel ⎦
19 cutting
20 advertising
21 marketing
22 no real intrinsic value
23 expensive
24 principal consumers
25 America ⎤ any order
26 Japan ⎦

Section 2
Task 2
1 Only so many people get married every year
2 *America*: People didn't know what they were
supposed to do when they got married – no
tradition.
 Japan: Japanese wanted to be more like westerners,
and part of the modern world.
3 *Japan* DeBeers designed an advertising campaign
identifying giving a diamond as a passport to
being modern.
4 *America*: Beginning of twentieth century
 Japan: 1963 or 1964
5 *Japan*: 0–65% of people giving diamonds, in 6
years.
6 *Japan*: Japan is now the second largest diamond
market outside USA.
25% of all diamonds are sold there.

Task 3
This exercise is mainly to increase awareness of different
styles of language according to whether it is spoken or
written and in a formal or informal context. Generally
speaking, Epstein's choice of words is the result of them
occurring in spontaneous, informal speech and, to some
extent to his style of American English. However, the
differences between formal and informal, spoken and
written do not make these words or phrases mutually
exclusive. The individual words are not always mutually
interchangeable, either, as their accepted meaning is often
derived from context.

'only so many people'
'just came along naturally'
'main motive'
'working on this assumption'
'a passport to being . . .'
'they found enormous response'
'practically zero'

Section 3
Task 2
The best summary is C.

UNIT 8
Section 1
Task 2
1 caterpillar 2 pupa/chrysalis 3a antenna
b wing c marking d wing span e adult butterfly.
Task 3
Text C tells you the most: It is from an advertising leaflet
for the butterfly farm.

Text A is an extract from the big glossy butterfly farm
catalogue.

Text B is an extract from an interview with the manager of
the farm.

As opposed to the written texts, Text B is one long
rambling sentence with a certain amount of repetition and

redundancy. The personal pronoun is used ('we collect')
instead of a passive (unlike in Text A). Vocabulary is
simple in contrast to words and expressions in A, e.g.
'hue', 'colourful vibrant wings', 'favours', 'by virtue of'.
More colloquial expressions, e.g. 'by the way', 'this is . . .'
are used.

There is some ambiguity in the last sentence of Text A.
Who does 'them' and 'their' refer to? The visitors?!

Section 2
Questionnaire
1 a 2 b 3 c 4 b 5 b 6 abcd
Tasks 1 and 2
See table on page 65.

Section 3
Task 3
Here today, gone tomorrow

You can help to save British butterflies.
Join the BBCS.
Plant your garden with butterfly-attracting flowers.
Create and maintain truly wild areas of habitat.
Report to us all threats to habitats.
Control the use of pesticides and herbicides.
Make a donation to the Society's Reserve Fund for the
management and purchase of butterfly reserves.

Picture letter	Family	Butterfly common name	Colours	Food	Size	Distribution	Habitat	Special notes
a	Brassolidae	Owl butterflies	Dark brown outside with a big 'eye', electric blue inside	Banana plant and bananas	Wing span 9–10″	S. America. Brazil esp.		Crepuscular (flies at dusk)
h	Danidae	Monarch	Orange and black	Milkweed		USA, S. America, C. America, Australia, New Zealand & Canaries		Long migration. Poisonous.
e	Heliconidae		Orange, black, red.	Passion flower	very long narrow wings	Central S. America & Florida		Poisonous.
g	Papilionidae	Swallow-tails	All the colours of the rainbow	Fennel (UK) Citrus (Far East)		Throughout the world	Deep jungle. Top of jungle canopy. Open, temperate areas. Marshland	All shapes, sizes & colours. With or without tails.
f	Pieridae	Cabbage white	White yellow sulphur	Cabbage		All over the world.		Live out in the open . . white to reflect excessive light
b	Lycaenidae	Blues, hairstreaks	Green blue red purple		Smallish		All sorts: trees, meadows . . .	Girate hind wings. Some have tails.
c	Morphidae		Electric blue		12″ wingspan	Only in Central S. America		Made into jewellery, etc.
d	Nymphalidae	Cracker	Gentle blues & greys		3½″ wingspan			Makes noise like static electricity
		Leaf	Leaf outside, orange & blue stripes inside					Clever defence mechanism ∴ looks like leaf

UNIT 9
Section 1
Task 2
1 a meal en route
2 arrival in Cairo
3 before leaving London
4 a guided sightseeing tour
5 an early stage of the journey
6 after the tour
7 the return journey
8 leaving London
9 arrival in London
10 approaching Cairo
11 a drive through the city

Task 3
1 a 2 c 3 b 4 a 5 c 6 c 7 c 8 a 9 b
10 a 11 c

Section 2
Task 2
a 'just saved up' 'lump sum'
b 'overwhelming' 'indulgence' 'barmy'
c 'worthwhile' 'barmy'
d 'your ears start to pop'
e 'has put me quite at ease' 'one-upmanship' 'flashy people'
f 'rather scared' 'lop-sided'

Task 4
See table below.

	What are their reasons for being on the trip?	How do they consider themselves?	What do their friends at home think?	What are their impressions of the trip?
Elderly woman from the south of England	Wanted to fly in Concorde, wanted to see the Pyramids and the Sphinx	–	Some thought she was crazy, but a lot are very envious and would like to have gone as well	Great, absolutely fantastic
Young woman from the south of England	The flight on Concorde:- an ambition and an indulgence	–	There are those who think she's barmy	Absolutely overwhelming. Everything it should be
Middle-aged man from the north-east of England	The flight on Concorde	–	They're all envious	Worth every penny
Middle-aged man from the south of England	Last week his wife spent about £1000 in Harrods, so this week he's doing the same sort of thing by going out for the day on Concorde	–	(They have no idea how much he's spending)	(Very quiet.) Worth the money
Young man from the south-west of England	His father fancied the idea, so he thought 'Why not?' It's a one-upmanship, once-in-a-lifetime thing.'	Not wealthy or flashy	–	The flight has put him quite at ease
Late middle-aged woman from the north-west of England	–	Not a rich person. Not an adventurous sort.	–	So fantastic, absolutely unbelievable

Section 3

Task 1

1 e 2 c 3 g 4 a 5 b 6 h 7 j 8 d 9 f
10 i

Task 4

Where are we at the moment?

And how high are we at the moment?

So we are still climbing?

Do you ever get used to flying this aircraft?

Is that really a bother, or is that something you enjoy?

And how do you get to fly a Concorde?

How much does the plane really fly itself?

Is that really necessary to have that label there?

What would happen if you could open that window?

We seem to be making a turn, now. Where are we now?

Section 4

Task 2

Advertisement:
Concorde 100 £795 champagne lunch dinner coach guide camel horse carriage tips Pyramid Holiday Inn 11.30 a.m. 10.30 p.m. 7

Route map:
London—Austrian Alps—Venice—Adriatic—Mediterranean—South of Crete—Cairo

Cairo map:
Twelfth-century citadel, River Nile, Pyramids of Cheops and Khafre, The Sphinx, Papyrus Museum, Pyramid Holiday Inn Hotel, Bazaar, President Sadat's Tomb

---

UNIT 10

Section 1

Task 2

1 Reassurance 4 13
2 Denial 3 15
3 Promise 2 9
4 Expressing an opinion 5 10
5 Warning 7 16
6 Paying a tribute 6 12
7 Resignation from a post 8 14
8 Acceptance of a post 1 11

Task 3

Although the function of an utterance may be made clear by looking at the structure used, it is generally only by taking context, voice range and intonation into account that we can be sure of what function the speaker really wants to convey.

If necessary ask students to listen to the extracts again, with the transcript, and try to identify where and how the function depends on structure, vocabulary, voice range, intonation and context.

Remind students that these features are all part of their spoken English, too, and they may not be the same as those they rely on in speaking and interpreting their native language.

Extract 1 (acceptance) 'I accept the nomination'
Extract 2 (promise) 'I'll never tell a lie. I'll never make . . . , etc'
Extract 3 (denial) 'I am not and never have been . . .'
Extract 4 (reassurance) repetition of same statement
Extract 5 (expressing an opinion) 'I believe that' 'I believe we should . . .'
Extract 6 (paying a tribute) context, vocabulary, tone of voice
Extract 7 (warning) 'If they *don't* (insistent intonation) . . . they're going to find . . .'
Extract 8 (resignation) 'I think it best that I remove myself . . .'
Extract 9 (promise) 'I shall return'
Extract 10 (expressing an opinion) 'I have a dream'
Extract 11 (acceptance) 'I take up this task' 'I accept your summons'
Extract 12 (paying a tribute) context, vocabulary, tone of voice
Extract 13 (reassurance) repetition of 'again' 'Your boys are not going to be sent . . .'
Extract 14 (resignation from a post) 'To continue . . . would . . .'
Extract 15 (denial) 'I am innocent of the charges against me'
Extract 16 (warning) Context . . . 'Our nation is moving towards two societies . . .'

Section 2

Task 2

There are eighteen proverbs in all.

Task 3

Silence is golden.
It never rains but it pours.
Lovely weather for ducks.
Look after the pennies and the pounds will look after themselves.
Everything comes to he who waits.
You can't believe everything you hear.
There's no smoke without fire.
You only get what you pay for.
Every cloud has a silver lining.
It's no use crying over spilled milk.
You could knock me down with a feather.

Task 5

1 You only get what you pay for.
2 Lovely weather for ducks
3 It's no use crying over spilled milk.
4 You can't believe everything you hear.
5 It never rains, but it pours.

Section 3
Tasks 2 and 3

	Adjectives	Notes
Poem	mocking (he and his brother) threatening (when father says phrase)	stress/rhythm and intonation '. . so we practise them in bed at night.'
Play man	impatient threatening	'Thére you are' (intonation)/'And high time, too.' Tone of voice/stress and intonation: 'It is <u>my</u> business, <u>my</u> girl'/'While <u>you're</u> living under <u>my</u> roof.'
girl	defiant	'You've got no right at all. Do you hear?' 'Réspect' (intonation)
Advertisement Voice 1	bored threatening superior	lack of voice range/intonation high-falling intonation, 'Eric, Eric' 'Sit down, will you!'/It is Eric, isn't it?/Sighs/Were you aware . . .?
Voice 2	polite pleasant nervous	'Thank you'/repetition of 'Sir' 'The Volvo, Sir?'/'I believe it is, Sir (rising intonation) voice range/hesitation/nervous laugh
Announcement	pleasant, happy, excited mysterious sad, nervous, distressed	voice range, exaggerated rising intonation speed of delivery, reduced voice range with rise fall intonation tone of voice, hesitation

TEXT OF THE RECORDINGS

UNIT 1
Section 1
Task 1   (0′59″)
Male guest Oh, I say. That looks delicious.
Female guest Oh!
Host Ah ha. One of my wife's specialities.
Hostess It's something I picked up in Morocco.
Male guest Ah!
Hostess Could you pass that to Penelope, Ted?
Female guest You must give me the recipe.
Hostess Well, you really need one of these to do it
  properly.
Female guest Oh?
Male guest What an amazing thing. I don't think I've
  seen one before. Have you, love?
Female guest No.
Hostess Oh, they're super. I just had to buy one. Have I
  given you enough? I got it in the market in Casablanca,
  terribly cheap. The rice is just there.
Female guest Oh huh.
Hostess Oh, I hope you like brown rice. We don't eat
  white rice any more.
Male guest Mm.
Hostess It was an awful thing to get back on the plane, of
  course, but it's been jolly useful.
Male guest Mm.
Hostess We use it all the time, don't we, darling?
Host Mm.
Hostess Oh, do come back for more.
Host It's called a tajine. The Moroccans use them all the
  time.
Female guest Oh.
Host Not the sort of thing you find in Woolworth's,
  though. (*Laughter*)
  Now, now, what about some wine?
Male guest Mm.
Host This is one we rather like.

Section 2
Tasks 1 and 4   (2′23″)
1 Good evening, it's so kind of you
  To have us here tonight.
  We didn't feel like coming
  But one has to be polite.

  My word! You really do look well,
  And younger every year.
  I feel I have to say that
  Since that's why you asked me here.

Chorus
  Dinner parties are frightfully super.
  Play your cards well and it's all fun and games.
  Dinner parties are frightfully super.
  Meet the right people and drop the right names.

2 Your children have grown up so fast
  They change each time we come.
  They look really intelligent.
  Though actually they're dumb.

  The little girl's just like her mum.
  The boy's just like his dad.
  If they keep growing up like this,
  Things will be pretty bad.

3 The coq au vin was quite superb.
  It tasted like old hen.
  I'd never had your cheesecake.
  And I don't want to again.

  I couldn't stand your homemade wine
  So I left it in the cup.
  Could you pass me the recipe for your ratatouille?
  So I can tear it up.

4 The conversation really flowed
  At least *you* never stopped.
  We couldn't get a word in
  So quite soon our interest dropped.

  The evening was quite splendid
  We've not laughed so much in years
  I'm sorry, we really must go now
  Thank God, I'm bored to tears.

Section 3
Task 2   (4′39″)
Interviewer So how did you come to write that song,
  Rene?
Rene Well I wrote it a few years ago after I'd been at a
  rather formal dinner party, sitting next to a crusty old
  stick, a lady I knew, and I thought 'This is going to be a
  bit of an effort', [Mmm] and I plucked up courage and
  started chatting to her about herself and she said she'd
  been in Egypt and various things. And I was following
  the line of the conversation and all of a sudden she
  stopped dead and looked at me and said: 'If you'd really
  like to know more about me I shall write out my
  curriculum vitae for you!' [Ooh] And I thought that was
  so rude after making that effort that I looked around and
  thought 'Well what are other people talking about?' And
  I realized that other people don't ask direct questions,
  it's one of the things, unwritten laws of social etiquette.
  You skirt the issue if you're trying to find out things, or
  you make polite niceties and nice noises at dinner

parties, but you don't often say what your emotions are doing underneath.

Interviewer [Hmm hm] Can I come back to something you said? You said something about erm people not asking direct questions, yeah? Why do you think that is?

Rene I think it's partly fear, that they feel that they themselves will be exposed if they're asked those questions, and there is some sense of losing face by showing too much of yourself. I think it might be a particularly British thing because I was for instance in the USA with people I'd never met before, went to a very large dinner party, and within seconds people were telling me what their psychiatrist had said about them and their problems with the grocer and so on. Things that nobody in England would open out and do because there is a fear, there is a protective barrier and a sense of inferiority for anybody who dares to disobey these social norms.

Interviewer [Hmm hm] Rene, when we talked about this song I think once before, you mentioned something about the way people don't listen to one another, and that was one of the reasons that you had written the song, you were very concerned about this.

Rene Certainly a lot of my songs are concerned with communication. I was initially very inspired by the works of Wesker and Pinter and Albee and the way they show the people talking past each other, through each other, at each other, but never really with each other, and this is something that in different ways I try to show in a lot of my songs. I even try and find the gulf between the Third World, the developing world, and our own world, because some of the things people talk about there miss each other by miles. And we do this in our own . . . unless you're really close to people and you have a total trust, [Mmm] very often you say things as much to defend yourself as to listen to them. You're so concerned with the kind of impression you ought to be making [Hmm hm] that you fail to be listening to what's coming back to you from them. We're all guilty of it.

Interviewer Right, especially in that situation.

Rene Very much so, and [Yeah] the more you know somebody, the more you relax and probably allow yourself to listen properly to them. [Hmm hmm] That does demand a lot more energy and a lot more time. Some people are so engrossed and stressed by the daily energy of living that they simply haven't got time to make space for another person's being within them.

Interviewer You mentioned your other songs just now What sort of other things do you write about in your other songs? What themes?

Rene Well one of the other themes I'm very concerned about is the use of time. I wrote one for instance about the fact that you give people flowers long after they're gone, and when people are leaving a firm that they've been working for, you give them a drink and say: 'What a jolly good fellow' and so on. But at the time they were there perhaps you'd never noticed them, never took the time again to listen to them properly. We always seem to be missing the mark as far as time goes. I hate the thought of time rushing past. I really want to live every single minute to the full. Some of the songs are expressing that. The fact that you never have anything but this second that you're living in, that when you're looking to the future or the past, that doesn't really exist at all. And yet a lot of us find it the hardest thing of all, to coincide with the second that we're living in.

Interviewer And well, perhaps a final question. Why do you write songs at all? Why songs? Why not poetry or novels or something else?

Rene It's something to do with a sense of rhythm. There's a terrifically enjoyable discipline about fitting into a nutshell your own thoughts. In a poem you've got more freedom, you're not restricted by the music. But music itself is a wonderful art form and it conveys emotion more directly than anything, to me anyway. More directly than painting. More directly than theatre or whatever. If I hear a piece of music, ooh that's it, instantly, in the heart. [Mmm] There's even music therapy and so on, [Right] which shows that it can do this. If one can convey by one's own creativity a mood in another person through the music, and then enhance it with a discipline of well-chosen words, then I think you've got a perfect portrait of an instant communication.

Interviewer That's lovely. Well I think it's a lovely song. Thank you very much.

Rene Thank you very much Jane.

UNIT 2

Section 1

Tasks 2 and 3 (1'50")

Interviewer Could you tell me how we should keep fit?

Dr Davis Well really what we should do is to try to erm keep fit all round. Now what do I mean by that? I mean er such things as keeping up our strength and our suppleness and our stamina. Now er you may say why do we need all three of those things? Well, erm strength is useful really just so that we erm don't strain muscles or pull ligaments and tendons when we suddenly have to do something er a bit energetic like lift a heavy suitcase or er perhaps er shift a wardrobe or even get out of a chair or a bath. Erm. Suppleness is important er obviously so that you can can bend and and move freely and reach things, again without injuring yourself. And stamina is particularly important so that you can sort of keep going without without losing breath so you have you have endurance. One other great plus about developing stamina is that if you er maintain your stamina over a period of years, it actually has an effect of protecting the heart against heart disease.

Interviewer So out of those three, which is the most important?

Dr Davis Well, it depends who you are and what you want to do. I mean, the the reason for keeping fit is to keep fit for your way of life, the life you choose. Now, you may say 'Well, if I choose to sort of flop about in an armchair all day watching telly, I don't need to keep very fit, do I?' Well, that's unfortunately not true because there are always times when you have to make a little bit of extra demand on your body. Erm by force of circumstance. You may have to suddenly lift something heavy or move something or may have to er run for a bus or whatever. In which case you could do yourself an injury and you may even actually erm harm something important, like your heart. So it is important to actually to try to keep your fitness a little bit ahead of the sort of erm way of life that you have. Just to give you . . . to push yourself just that little bit harder and get yourself just that little bit fitter.

Section 2

Task 2 (3′25″)

Interviewer So how do you do it?

Dr Davis Well it doesn't have to be all grim and irksome. I mean, people have this view of fitness er freaks you know, who sort of are jogging grim-faced round the park you know, or who are er working weights, doing all sorts of horrible exercises you know, PT . . . Very grim indeed. It doesn't have to be like that. To keep yourself fit, or get yourself fitter, which is really what it's about, you just have to do a little bit more each day, erm or even every other day for that matter. By a little bit more I mean erm for instance just er walking a bit more often, a bit further, perhaps getting off the bus a stop or two sooner. Erm perhaps er doing a bit of a bit of cycling instead of travelling by public transport. Using the stairs instead of going up in the lift. It's surprising the number of people that erm I see on the London tube who are actually standing on the escalators going down you know, just standing there slowly going down. And the same with lifts. People who take the lift down I mean, that's ridiculous. You should at least walk down, but preferably walk up, because by walking upstairs you actually perform really quite a useful aerobic exercise, that's an exercise that develops stamina, and that's having a beneficial effect on your whole body, toning you up and helping to protect against heart disease.

Interviewer So it isn't necessary to play squash three times a week, or go swimming three times a week?

Dr Davis It isn't necessary. Er actually swimming is a rather good way of keeping fit because it's particularly excellent for erm all three of the S-Factors if you like, the strength, the suppleness and the stamina. It helps to develop all three of those rather well, and er it's also a very pleasant and relaxing way to keep yourself in shape. Three times a week would be just about right actually, or even twice a week, or even once a week. Em. Squash though is not a good way to get fit. You have to actually get fit to play squash. Squash is a very demanding game. A very very er energetic game, and in fact you could do yourself a lot of damage by playing squash if you're not in good physical shape to start with.

Interviewer I have a lot of friends who play sport, and they always seem to have bad backs and pulled tendons, so what would you say to them?

Dr Davis I'd say to them they're they're going about it the wrong way. Erm. They're forcing themselves into into sports, perhaps before they're ready, before they've got themselves in shape first. You have to get in shape to play these sports. Erm. And also for people who force themselves into these things generally. That's bad. Mustn't do that. Whenever you're exercising, or or just carrying out some physical activity, never push yourself beyond comfort. Anything that's uncomfortable, don't do it. Stop. Slow down. It's basically got to be fun. I mean, to keep yourself in shape you've got to carry on exercising week in week out, month in month out, year in year out. Now that sounds awful, but if you choose something which you enjoy doing, er, it's fun, then you will keep it up. You see you can't put fitness in the bank as it were. If you don't carry on exercising, all the benefits that you get from exercising will all disappear within about 6 to 8 weeks. All go and you'll be back where you started so you have to keep it up, and to keep it up, it has to be something you enjoy, it has to be fun. So choose something which you get a lot of pleasure out of, and that way it won't seem irksome at all.

Interviewer What do you do to keep fit?

Dr Davis Ah well, I'm glad you asked me that question. Actually, what I . . . I live in London and I work in London, er so what I what I do to keep fit is to certainly do quite a lot of walking. I certainly walk upstairs er a lot, but also I do a fair amount of cycling, er and as I'm dashing round London I I use the bike. I find it the fastest way to get around town and it's er it's really good for keeping in shape. I'm a little worried about the traffic fumes, I have to admit, but actually er it makes me feel very good to cycle around there and I get there on time!

Section 3

Tasks 1 and 2 (2′26″)

Interviewer I'm Michael Van Stratton. Thanks for joining me on 'Body Talk'. You're going to be helping me to help you lead healthier, fitter and more active lives. The reason we're doing this programme is because we've had an enormous response on the Nightline Alternative Medicine programme from you, the listeners. We'll be taking your letters to the experts and getting their opinion, as well as mine on how to make you lead more fulfilled and healthier lives for the whole family. We couldn't really start a new series on health matters without consulting the queen of health, Mrs Barbara Cartland.

Barbara Cartland Well at 83 I can tell you quite frankly, it's vitamins. If I didn't have vitamins, I wouldn't be able to go on doing what I'm doing, and I do take a lot because I've—there's a lot of me and a lot of old age to keep off. I do feel frightfully well. And I do find that every day I'm at home I can dictate 6–7,000 words, which is one chapter. You must keep active. If you don't keep active then you gradually decay.

Interviewer Do you think that what you eat is important, as well as taking the vitamins?

Barbara Cartland Well I think it's very important. I think the main thing is to avoid things like white bread and white sugar. We all know that. And I think you need er not so much food, but you need what I call proper nourishing food. But don't you see, pure food, vitamins are only pure food. People always talk as though they're some magic medicine. They're not. They're just pure food in a capsule. And it's just the same as going to the er—an aeronaut takes his food in a capsule.

Interviewer Barbara, if you were going to say in in a nutshell to our listeners the the Barbara Cartland sentence of how to keep fit and healthy. What would it be?

Barbara Cartland Oh, the two things which I go by. One is 'You are what you eat' and 'You become what you think'. And if you think that out, it's very very true, especially 'You become what you think'. If you think beastly horrible ghastly thoughts, you become a beastly horrible person, and if you don't eat the right things, well then you're ill and then you're horrible anyway, because everybody's disagreeable when they feel ill.

Interviewer Barbara, I hope we can come back to you er in ten years time and get your tips on how to survive to over 90.

Barbara Cartland Oh no, I hope not Michael. I think a li—enough's enough . . . of even of me!

UNIT 3

Section 1

Task 2 (0′24″)

For pleasure, 'cause it's fun. You can, er, figure out more things that you haven't learned.

For education, for . . . for everything. (laughs)

To know mo-, a bit more about life and science things and other things that you don't know yet.

When you're bored, when you're . . . when you don't have anything to do on Saturday nights, on Saturday mornings. When your parents are sleeping. For everything.

Section 1

Task 4 (3′47″)

Teacher I think there are a lot of reasons why it's good for children to read. Er . . . Not just reading for pleasure, but all of the subjects, no matter what subject it is, involve some reading, even if it's just art. [Mmm.] They have to read the directions to do an art project, and . . . ah. Social Studies they have to read. Science they have to read. And the more they read, ah, the easier, ah, the more their vocabulary will expand, and the better the . . . they'll do in their other subjects.

Erm . . . Also for, for pleasure, erm, es-, er, especially here in Puerto Ordaz where there aren't very many things to do. In- . . . instead of being out doing something they shouldn't be doing, ah, they can choose reading as a hobby.

Erm . . . It also improves their language tremendously. I can read a composition that a student has written that has, that reads a lot and I know, er, that he reads a lot by his use of the language and his vocabulary and a lot of advanced sentence structure that someone of that age normally would not, er, be able to handle.

Erm . . . What else? Erm . . . Sometimes children who have very limited experiences, whose families don't get out very much, er, maybe not have enough money, er, ah, just stay at home a lot, have real limited experiences and by reading they can expand their experiences about what happens in the world and I've had children who, in a reader, see a picture, an exercise and they see a picture of a lion and they don't know what it is, because either their parents haven't read to them, or they haven't read books, or they haven't been out. And if they haven't been to a zoo to see an actual lion they could have read in a book, or had their parents read to them about, er, lions. And they miss the, the problem, because they may, once you tell them what it is, explain, they they can do the exercise, but because they didn't know, didn't have the experience, they weren't able to do it.

Erm . . . er . . . For survival later, too. If you can't read, erm, a cook-book or a, a manual to, to repair things, you're lost in that you have to rely on someone else to, always. And you're not, er, independent.

Interviewer What is it good for children to read?

Teacher I think children should read everything, that, er, not just limit it to mystery books, or just to science fiction. In fact there are some children who, who say, 'No, no. I just want to read science fiction,' but, er, I think they should read, er, from different areas. Er . . . The newspaper, magazines. The School subscribes to, even though it's a small school, we've gotten in the budget approved to have fifteen magazines come in, and during their Silent Sustained Reading time can read magazines.

Erm . . . if . . . Anything that's written down, I think they should read. Whether a sign or newspaper, textbook, everything, and not just limit it to one or two things.

Erm . . . I think a lot of parents disagree that children, they say if they're reading comic books they're wasting their time, but if I have a child who's a poor student, if he'll read a comic book, er, I'm happy because he's reading something. Or if he's, while he's eating breakfast he's reading the back of the cereal box he's still reading something and I wouldn't take it away from him and say, 'Stop wasting your time,' because that is a step to go on to further reading and if you limit it to certain areas, then that will, it sometimes, it will stifle them and they'll stop reading completely. And they'll say, 'If I can't read the comic book then I don't want to read anything.' But reading the comic book could, erm, they say, 'Well I enjoyed this and I understood this, er, I think I'll try something else,' and that expands their reading. And they *can* learn something from a comic book.

Erm . . . It's also important, erm, if a student, if, a lot of the kids want to play games and they don't, it's a new game they don't know how to play, if they can't read the instructions, then they won't be able to play the game. Or, if they have a new toy, erm, if they can't read the instructions, they could possibly break the toy, and, by not learning how to use it properly.

Section 2

Tasks 2 and 3 (5′15″)

1 Yes, I like, when . . . I don't like when they kiss and when they take so much time kissing and putting make-up so much and then putting lipstick, yuk! It goes . . .
It's horrible . . . I don't like to see it.
Is it, is it the, the [It's terrible] too grown up, grown up?
Yeah, too grown up.
It's boring.
If they're kissing somewhere that no-one can see them, I think. Where it's not . . . I don't like it when it's a book about kissing right in front of everyone . . . nookie . . . I don't like it.
I think it probably better on the cheek, on the- kisses on the cheek, than on any other parts of the body.

2 Er . . . What goes upstairs black and white, and downstairs black and white and read? [I don't know]. A newspaper.
Rhymes like: I went swimming and the rim of the sw, of the swimming pool, which was very cool . . .
To laugh. To, to enjoy the book.
And to, to ex-, to tell it to other people.
If you're in a bad temper.

3 How they live and what part are they living. And, er, like that cactus. How can you, how, if, er, that, they, the roots grow up the, the place where the rain comes, comes back to them.
All kinds of things. Like you can cut up a cactus and you can get water.
Because it's about nature and I like nature.
Erm . . . 'Cause you can get, er, like oil, or things like that, you know, or juice, or something. [Mmm].
Like, erm, honey.
Because if, maybe if you get lost in the jungle and some forest you might need flowers, because they can help you. You can eat the petals, and you can, you can eat stuff, it depends if they're poisonous they help you survive.
Flowers and trees I'm not interested in.

4 Erm . . . Devils . . . Ooooh!
People walking into a haunted house.
Aha . . . Getting eaten-up by skeletons. [Or by goblins].
No, they get eaten by bats or see blood half of the time there's blood or they come in horrible things.
Monsters and stuff like that scare me. (They mostly scare me when they're going to bite someone.)
And this earthly ghostbuster . . . funny, funny.
No. No, no. Funny horrid stories, I mean. Like, erm . . . the bat runs into the, it runs into the, into a wall and then a devil comes out. Something like that.
A full-moon night. [Because the werewolves come out.]
Because . . .
They can see more, a bit . . . They can see a bit, not too much.
And it's dark and no-one can see and what's going to happen, and when it's dark and when you see at night you start getting more . . . [Scary. And it's quiet.] Right. Then suddenly comes attack!

5 Erm . . . I know it's not the animals that are talking, but I know it's the author, but I like to hear their feelings and . . . so then if I see an animal doing the same thing (. . .) then I know how they feel.
Yeah. That's pro . . . that's probably true.
They have all kinds of interesting colours. They do interesting things and . . . They do weird things. They look weird and . . . They have unusual things. (Mmm).
Like all kinds of animals that know how to make tricks.
Like dogs . . . er . . . monkeys and, all kinds of things.
It's probably (I don't think they're real stories.) stories.
It's just explaining about . . . (about animals. Like what can do and all that sort of things).

6 Rhyming ones and un-rhyming ones.
Erm . . . Some, they don't, they, they're not made the same. They're not, er . . . They don't sound the same.
My father owns a butcher's shop,
My mother cuts the meat,
And I'm the little dog,
That runs around the street.
I say the girls read more.
I say the read more.
All the boys I know don't really, most of them don't really like rhyme.
I get a lot of inspiration from . . .
What do I do? What do I do?
This library book is 42 years overdue.
I admit that it's mine,
but I can't pay the fine.
Should I turn it in,
or hide it again?
What do I do? What do I do?

7 They're exciting. They always have adventure and everything. It's a combination of all kinds of books.
Can be fantasy mystery. Er . . . [kissing] History mystery. Because you have to answer the mystery at the end. Not, no you don't have to answer it, but you can kind of answer it yourself.
Makes you want to get to the end.
Sometimes, way that, you don't have to read the end.
You just can . . . er . . . you just have to look carefully at the clues and, if you really pay attention to the clues, you can figure out who it is.
Erm . . . Who did something, Like, er, who killed someone.
You have to find, er, person has to find out who killed . . . police.
Sometimes, if you really look carefully at the clues it gives you, you can find out, maybe.
It's, er, sometimes about treasures, or robbery, or er, er, kidnapping.

Section 3

Tasks 1 and 3 (4′36″)

Interviewer 'In fairy tales,' Roald Dahl's book begins, 'witches always wear silly hats and black cloaks and they ride on broomsticks, but this is not a fairy tale. This book is about real witches.' As Roald Dahl told me, real witches don't look any different from other women and that's what makes them so dangerous.

Roald Dahl It's the same with spies, or murderers, or anything else. If you think that you are just a face in the crowd and you don't know who is the murderer, or who is the spy, er, equally, you don't know who is the witch amongst all the ladies in the world.

Interviewer We could have witches living next door, but not recognize them, because they look just like any other lady?

Roald Dahl Absolutely. And what makes them frightening, of course, is that witches have only one purpose in life, which is to kill children. Do away with them. Wipe them out. Er, slowly and gently, but, er, with, without ever being caught, because they work with magic. And all this is, er, it's explained in the book. Er, it's got to be plausible, it's got to be spooky and the child's really got to think that this is a threat.

Interviewer Are you giving them some helpful advice about how they can save themselves if there is a witch next door, or if their teacher is a witch?

Roald Dahl Very much so. Yes. You give them all the advice you possibly can, but, in the end, that advice isn't enough, you know. There's no such thing as saving a child from a witch, because, if they are after you, there's, there's virtually no way of getting them. The narrator in this particular book, which is me, gets caught in the end, you know. I won't say what what happens to me, but it is something awful and horrible. An, and, er, there's nothing you can do about it.

Interviewer In the evening, sometimes, do you think that there may be children all over the country, all over the world perhaps, unable to get to sleep because they're so frightened by what they've been reading in a book like this?

Roald Dahl Yes. I love that. Yes. Of course, it's, it's a lovely feeling. But mainly they're laughing, you know, which is an even better feeling.

Interviewer There's no doubt, of course, that Roald Dahl knows exactly what children love: They love to be scared, they love to laugh and they love to be rude.

Roald Dahl In my book *The BFG* there's a daring chapter in there about, er, breaking wind.

Interviewer 'Whiz-popping'.

Roald Dahl Yes. 'Whiz-popping'. And, er, that knocks them out, because they've never in, in polite company, or at school, or wherever, the, er, teacher, . . . they've never been allowed to talk about, er, farting, as we call it, er, and suddenly, if the teacher's reading the book, she's got a whole chapter on this one subject. And, and that knocks them out, you see. Er, but you've got to dare to do it.

Interviewer Magic, as well, must be an important ingredient to you.

Roald Dahl Magic is, yes. It's a lovely list to make. You've only just mentioned it and put it in my mind, but the list of, of the secret ingredients of a really good children's book are, er, magic and laughter and a spookiness; making them shiver and, of course, a very strong plot running all the way through.

Interviewer Roald Dahl is always bang up to date with

what children like best in his stories because they write to him every day.

Roald Dahl We're flooded, in this house, with letters. An, and I have, er, a patient, expert secretary who deals with piles of them every morning. And I do my very best, before I go up to work, between, I go up to work at 10 o'clock and, and from 9 to 10, or from 8.30 to 10, I read through the children's letters. And you get a wonderful idea of what hits them hardest, you know. And, I can see . . . Up to a year ago it was always *Charlie and the Chocolate Factory*, or *Danny the Champion of the World*, or *James the Giant Peach* and, suddenly, *The BFG* has taken over. Er, it was my thirteenth children's book and I think it's my best and I think, I hope, anyway, that *The Witches* is on a par with *The BFG*.

Interviewer Does it make you cross that people seem to think that writing for children is really quite easy?

Roald Dahl Oh, terribly cross, yes. It is awfully easy to write a mediocre book for children. It's easier than to write a mediocre novel. First of all, it's a little shorter, usually, you know. But I'm absolutely certain that it is harder to write a first-rate, enduring book for children than it is to write a first-rate, enduring novel. (7'36")

Interviewer Eric Carle was born in the United States in 1929, but when he was only just out of nursery school his parents decided to move the family back to their native Germany. The rigidity and harshness of his school days there are still very fresh in Eric Carle's memory.

Eric Carle I hated school. It's as simple as that. The first week of what was to be the beginning of my education in Germany I received corporal punishment; three in each hand, for a minor thing. We were at the City Health Department for a physical examination at the beginning of school. The phone rang and and the doctor was not in the office. And I lifted it up. And the teacher came in and said 'Who did it? You report to me afterwards'. And he beat me up.

Interviewer How old were you at that time?

Eric Carle Six. And, er, here was this tiny, little kid; just had come from United States; barely spoke German and I thought that's what you do with phones. You lift phones if somebody's not in. Well, you don't do that. See? So, looking back at that I know I turned off. I don't know how, how I went through school. I hated school until I went to art school. Then I began to breathe again.

Interviewer Do you think the kind of books that you're producing now would've helped the six-year-old Eric Carle?

Eric Carle Yes, I think that's part of why I do books. Books for the six-year-old Eric Carle. With my books I try to be half a toy and half a book. And it is for the child that is leaving home and going to school. At home it's the toys, the warmth of the home and all those things. And then the child goes to school and there are books and desks and discipline and so forth. So with these books, with the holes and the folds, I create, try to create a toy that you can read and a book you can play with.

Interviewer How does an idea for a book develop in your mind? For instance, *The Very Hungry Caterpillar*, which is probably your best known book. Where did that idea come from? How did it grow as you devised the book?

Eric Carle It started out with a stack of papers. I punched holes in it; I looked at it, I was not thinking in terms of a book, just playing around. Punched these holes in a book stack of papers and I said 'Oh, this could be a book-worm'. That's how it all started. And, er, the worm didn't seem right. And it was a green worm in the beginning and it didn't seem right. But, anyway, er, that's how it began.

Interviewer Why do you think that book's been such a huge success?

Eric Carle Oh, that's the wrong question. I would like to commission somebody to find out why it is, so successful. I really don't know. It's as simple as that. I've given it a lot of thought. Of course the story of the caterpillar and the butterfly has occupied the minds of poets way back into antiquity. Maybe that is an element of the success; almost something archetypal. I don't know.

Interviewer There's a lot of humour in the story too, isn't there. I can remember my two-year-old son, before he could really recognize the letters, could read that book of yours to himself. Turning over the pages he knew the rhythm of the story and getting to a line like 'That night he had a stomach-ache' would roar with laughter.

Eric Carle Yes.

Interviewer That's part of the enjoyment of it.

Eric Carle Yes. I think with children, when it comes to humour you have to have an outrageous humour. You cannot be subtle. The child is not so sure whether you are humorous or serious. So, I think *The Caterpillar* has this outrageous, nonsensical humour. The child doesn't have to think; doesn't have to worry, you know. 'It is humour. I don't have to figure this out. It is humour'.

Interviewer Always, in your stories, there are several things to learn. As well as the actual enjoyment of the story, as you're reading it; you learn to tell the time; you learn the days of the week; colours; counting. (Aha) Are those elements important to you in the story? They must be.

Eric Carle They're number one as far as I'm concerned, but in the presentation, in the way they are in the book; very often camouflaged and secondary. The clock in the ladybird book is very small. It is for the child who's interested in, in time, who would find find the clock and, with the help of the teacher, or the parent, learn about time. For the child who's not interested in the time, that child can ignore it. There's always a level an emotional level in there, somehow. And I think that's where a lot of books for young children fail, in that they try to teach, only. And, what they, in fact, do, is turn off. So I avoid this with colour, with humour, with stories, with learning and the child is free to choose his or her level.

Interviewer From time to time Eric Carle likes to visit schools and meet groups of young children. Rather than simply reading to them, he shows them how a book is created.

Eric Carle When I'm in a classroom I say 'When I was your age, I had an Uncle August and he was a story-teller. And I'd go to my uncle August and say "Tell me a story." And he'd say "You have to wind up my thinking machine".' That's how we'd start out. And I tell the children to wind up their thinking machine and then I say 'I've an idea for a book. It's about your favourite animals. What's your favourite animal? "Cat".' I draw a cat. 'What's your favourite animal? "Giraffe".' I put a giraffe neck on. 'What's your favourite? "Turtle".' I put a turtle back on. So I involve them. Then, when it's finished I say 'Now, this is the cover for the book. What's missing? Oh, the title is missing. What do we call this?' Get all kinds of crazy names. So when this is finished I say 'We have the title page, the title, and the author's name'. The author is always the children because they've told me what to do. And then I say 'Well, I did the picture', and I sign it. I say 'Now we have a cover'. Then I bring out, er *The Mixed-up Chameleon*. I say '*The Mixed-up Chameleon* was done in that fashion'. It's really not completely true, but this they can relate to. And then I will read the Chameleon book to them. See now they know how a book is done, where the ideas come from.

Interviewer Yes, that's a lot of fun for the children. It's al, always animals, incidentally, isn't it? Children love animals and love the colours and the adventures and the movement of animals, which come over so vividly in your pictures.

Eric Carle Very often small animals too. I like small animals. I think, er, I think children feel very insignificant, small, helpless. It's tough to be small at times. And if a little caterpillar can turn into a butterfly, maybe they can turn into a butterfly. And if a little chameleon can change shape, maybe they can change shape.

Interviewer You have a new book *The Very Busy Spider* coming out before long. Can you describe that one for me?

Eric Carle I do like little animals, little insects, and I have been watching spiders, of course. I live in the country. So, three years ago I knew I wanted to do a book about a spider. That's about all I knew and I did a little drawing of a spider and a little spider web and I stuck it above my work table. And I looked at it for a while. I worked at it. I put it away. I worked at it. It seemed good. It seemed bad. It didn't seem right. I shouldn't do it. I should do it. That kind of process. I usually make up about fifty dummies: Thirty-two page dummies then I quickly sketch in my story. It's very important for a story to flow right. It has to be composed almost like a piece of music, I think. And you don't do just picture, picture, picture. It has to flow right so that was the process with the spider, too. And then my books have holes and things and 'What am I going to do here?' It was almost a logical conclusion, wasn't it? To wind up with a touchable spider web.

Interviewer So what happens as you turn the pages of the book is that you can feel the web of the spider and the spider itself.

Eric Carle Yes. The central elements of the story: The spider, the fly and the web can be touched. The other animals cannot be touched.

Section 3
Task 4

1 1st boy Well, it's by Ronald Dahl and it's called *George's Marvellous Medicine*. Well, um, George's mum and dad go out for . . . an . . . couple of hours and George is sent to his grandma's, and she is, um, she's not very nice to him. She's, she's, um, she nags him. 'Go and get my pills. Go and get everything.' And then when her pills run out, he's sent up to the chemist. And while, and he gets her pills and he gets loads of other things, like soap, um, toothpaste, and he mixes them all together and then as she drinks it, she goes flying straight through the roof and, um, they have to get a crane to pull her out of the roof. And, um, then he mixes some more. And number 2 goes completely wrong 'cos, er, just their body grows. Number 3 their head grows long and number 4, it makes them shrink. But grandma thought number 4 was her drink so she drank it and she shrunk and she shrunk and she shrunk. They said, 'Stop. You're just about the right size.' But then she kept shrinking and she shrunk and she shrunk and she shrunk. And so, in the end, she's about half an inch tall and, um, George's mum has a go at him and his dad and George is sent to his room for the rest of the day and it shows on the back cover a hen looking at his medicine, just about to take some of it. And I thought this was a really good book. It's very funny.

(4 versions of Roald Dahl story)   (1′45″)

2 1st girl Well, his gran's horrible and he doesn't really like her and she has to have this medicine every day. So he decides to go to the, um, make a potion for her. So he goes to the shed and he gets all the things from there, like cow medicines and things like that and he mixes it all up into a bowl and he gives it to his gran and she shoots up into the air through the ceiling. And she stays up there and she cracks through the roof of the things. She stays up there and when the father comes home, they give some . . . they give . . . they make . . . try to make a different potion and they give it to the animals on their farm and all the animals grow different sizes and they turn purple and things. They, they try to make it . . . and . . . in the end they . . . they find the right potion again.

Woman What happens to grandma?

1st girl Well, she comes down again. She shrinks though and she shrinks into a little ball and she's never seen again.

(1′06″)

3 2nd boy Well, it's about, um, this family that live on the farm and their grandma lives with them, and they . . . one day his mum, his dad's working and his mum goes off to do the shopping and his nan's all fine about George when his mum's about but when she goes out, she starts being really horrible to him. And she was snapping and getting him really scared and he was . . . and he . . . and she looks like a witch and he was getting really scared and she was saying, 'Bring in this medicine.' And, um, so he, he decided to make up this medicine and just get everything and pile it in and boil it up. And she was, she was nagging on at him for it and he just made it up and then he, um, gave it to her and she went all funny, and she started to tall and she grew as tall as the . . . she grew out of the ceiling, and, um, then she grew out of the house. And when his dad came back, he saw this. Well, first he gave it all, he gave it . . . some to the animals and then his dad comes home and he says 'we would make millions out of this'. So he tries to make a factory but things went wrong. It ended when, er . . . um, it didn't work out and then I think, um, er, I think his grandma went back to normal size 'cos he gave her, he rever . . ., he reversible medicine 'cos they done something wrong. I really enjoyed it. I've read it quite a few times.

(1′35″)

4 2nd girl Well, it's all about this boy and one day his mum and dad go out and he sort of doesn't like his granny and she's always wanting this medicine. And one day he goes to get her medicine and he has a brilliant idea and he goes up to the bathroom and things and he gets all these things and mixes 'em together. And when he comes down and he's mixed all these horrible things, like, um, soap and things, he comes down and he gives it to her and she suddenly grows big and she goes out of the roof and then he . . . she gives it to all the other animals and everything goes big. Um, his mum and dad come back and, and she goes through the roof and the gran comes right on the roof and they find out.

Woman She gets so big, she goes through the roof?

2nd girl Yeh.

Woman And then what happens?

2nd girl Goes through to the attic as well and then they feed it to all the farm animals and they grow big. I think she goes back to normal again in the end.

(0′59″)

UNIT 4

Section 1
Task 1   (0′59″)
(silent movie music)

Section 1
Task 2   (5′41″)
(extracts from film soundtracks)

Section 2
Tasks 1 and 2   (3′08″)

First woman All right, well, I'll tell you what I don't like about them. Well, one of the things I don't like about them is that they're full of men for a start. There are very, very few women characters and the men are all terribly macho, sort of doing what a man's gotta do type thing. All terribly heroic, lots of action and the women, basically, I think, are. Well, there are two types. Either they're sort of the heroine in love with the hero, basically, sort of pretty pathetic and um totally unable to cope by herself and needing the man to come in and bail her out. And in the end everything's fine because the man has sort of helped her and she's um she's managed to do whatever it was she couldn't do without him. Right – and if they're not that type then, then they're the sort of gangster's moll in the saloon. Um, usually a very strong sort of personality, very sexy, er, but they often get shot in the end because they're, they're wicked and they're threatening in some way and because they're strong they don't survive the film. They get bumped off. So that's really why I don't like them. I feel they're very macho.

Second woman Well, I, I think maybe we've been watching different types [laugh] of the same film because what I like about this er particular type of film. I like the ones that are, er, if you like, work against the genre, so what I quite, the ones that I like best actually set up the stereotypes and then undermine them. Um, but I have to say that the stereotype does kind of appeal to me in a rather vicarious self-indulgent kind of way. I mean I rather like, OK, I do actually find the idea of the kind of lone hero who is against society quite attractive. Um, I like the idea of the sort of self-sufficient, competent man. I mean, it is, I agree with you it is generally a man, um, who comes in and kind of saves the day. I suppose that that appeals to something quite, um, you know, one of, one of my sort of fantasies. Um, and I like indulging that. Um, I don't like, I don't like the violence. I don't like the really violent ones. I don't mind the stereotyped violence, that's, that I can handle quite well. But the ones that I really like are the ones that as I say kind of undermine the stereotype somewhat. So the ones that I like are things like *Hombre*. Have you seen *Hombre*? [No – I haven't seen that.] OK. Well in *Hombre* you have the, the lone silent sort of character who is immensely competent, immensely efficient but he's the man who identifies with the underdog. He identifies with the Indians because he's brought up with them. Um, and er, and he challenges all the sort of the general prevailing myths of the kind of supremacy of the white man and the white man's values and that kind of thing.

First woman Right, because, in fact, that's another thing I very much object to – the way that all Indians are always portrayed like that. [Right, well I also object to that.]

Second woman That's right. I object to that very much but I like, I love the humour in them. I love the humour of the genre. I love the, er, one-off lines.

UNIT 5
Section 1
Task 2 (2′18″)
1 . . . and threatened to set fire to it if his demands were not met. He was later overpowered by security men, posing as cleaners, when they stopped to refuel in Miami.
2 They were all allowed home after treatment for the effects of smoke, but one asthmatic passenger was detained and was said to be in a 'poorly' condition. The incident caused delays to several early morning services operating out of Victoria Station.
3 . . . the top international watchdog body on dope warned today. Trafficking and abuse are so pervasive that entire economies are disrupted, legal institutions menaced and the very security of some states threatened.
4 . . . by smashing a French window at the rear. The haul included a horse-shoe brooch with diamonds set in platinum, a silver pill-box, three Georgian perfume bottles and two silver penknives.
5 . . . reported smelling it just after 8 am. They immediately sent out a service engineer, but he didn't arrive in time. 73-year-old Mrs. Elizabeth Dodd, who was brewing a cup of tea at the time, was trapped in the wreckage of her ground-floor kitchen before being rescued by neighbours.
6 . . . the two men were cut from the wreckage of their car by firemen, but were both dead on arrival at hospital. They were later named as Mr. John O'Brien of Glendale Avenue, Moss Side and Mr. Andrew Mitchell of Heath Street, Cheadle. Both men were fitters for the Gas Board.
7 Dolland pleaded guilty to attacking a girl in the city-centre on the night of January 13th, in an attempt to get money to buy heroin. Judge William Booth told him, 'As far as this court is concerned, the taking of drugs by criminals cannot be a source of mitigation'.
8 . . . just as he was about to enter the inner door of the bank Gill ran up and tried to grab the bag. However the security man held on to it and Gill ran away. The bag contained cheques and cash belonging to a nearby garage.

Section 2
Tasks 1 and 2 (2′57″)
It's 12 noon and here are this lunch-time's main stories.
(a) The work-to-rule by air-traffic controllers is now affecting the majority of Britain's   . Some 75% of all flights leaving Heathrow Airport this morning were   , and it was a similar story at Gatwick, Manchester, Glasgow and Edinburgh. Passengers bound for European   were the worst hit. A British Airways spokesman claimed that they were managing to clear a backlog of breakfast-time   by mid-morning, but such large-scale delays were causing havoc with schedules for later flights because   were in the wrong place at the

wrong time. The spokesman praised passengers for the great   they have shown so far. The outlook for those   today or tomorrow, at least, is not very cheerful. However, the   say that passengers should check-in for flights as normal, at the advised times. The controllers, who began their action at midnight last night, are   against what they claim to be inadequate and potentially dangerous manning levels at the country's main air-traffic control centres.

(b) Latest Government   show a slight improvement in the unemployment situation. The number of registered unemployed fell by just over 12,000 last month; the first   there has been in the total, this year.

The Opposition, however, claim that when the number of   who left the register to return to colleges and universities is taken into account, there was a substantial   in the number of long-term unemployed. Mr. Eric Watkins the Shadow Employment Spokesman, said that today's figures   a totally unrealistic picture of the unemployment situation. 'There is no real   in unemployment, nor in the suffering and misery of thousands of families in this country', said Mr. Watkins. He called on the Government to take positive   , in next month's Budget, towards revitalising the depressed

(c) Police in North London are looking for a gang of armed   who got away with over £¼ million-worth of   in a raid on a Hampstead jeweller's this morning. Staff who arrived to   the shop at 8:30 were held at gun-point by the gang, who proceeded to empty display cabinets and the safe. They made their   in a white Jaguar car which was later found abandoned in nearby Finchley.

(d) Three men   and a woman and child were seriously injured in an   which happened on the A11 near Norwich. Their car was in a head-on collision with an articulated   . The lorry driver escaped with minor   and was released from hospital in Norwich after treatment for cuts and bruises. Police are appealing for   to the accident, which happened at about 7:30 this morning.

Section 3

Task 2   (2′09″)

–And now over to Nick with the latest update on the traffic situation.

–Thanks Andy. Well, there's a bit of a headache for drivers coming into the city-centre this morning. First of all, a serious accident has completely blocked the A6, Chapel Street, in Salford, between Bridge Street and Blackfriars Street. There are already long tail-backs of traffic there and the police say the road won't be open again for another hour or so. Drivers should use Liverpool Road to come into the city-centre from the Salford area. Once again, that's an accident blocking the A6, Chapel Street, between Bridge Street and Blackfriars Street, in Salford. Another emergency, this time in John Dalton Street in the centre of town, er where a fire has meant the closing of the road and has also led to restricted access to Albert

Square and the southern end of Cross Street, down there near the Town Hall. Avoid that area if you possibly can; it looks like things are pretty snarled up there. John Dalton Street, at the junction with Cross Street and Albert Square; there's a fire, causing serious congestion and delays, of course.

Er, Meanwhile, in Cannon Street, things are pretty wet outside the Cathedral, because . . . yes, you've guessed it, there's a burst water main. The Water Authority gentlemen are all out there in their wellingtons, but the road is, in fact, closed to traffic. That's Cannon Street closed between Deansgate and Corporation Street, due to a burst water main.

And whilst we're talking about pipes under the ground, just a reminder that the sewer-reconstruction work is still going on in Great Ancoats Street, in Ancoats, with traffic being diverted into Henry Street on the east side of Great Ancoats Street, between Oldham Road and Ancoats.

And, finally, there are roadworks starting today in Mosley Street, in the city-centre, between Princess Street and Piccadilly Gardens. This section of Mosley Street will be reduced to single-lane traffic controlled by temporary traffic-lights and delays are expected. The work is due to last at least a fortnight. So, try to avoid Mosley Street, if you're in a hurry and, especially, at peak times.

Well, not a very happy picture on the roads in central Manchester this morning, I'm afraid. British Rail report no problems on the trains this morning, however, and things are running smoothly down at the airport, too. We'll have another update on the road situation, after the News, at 9. Meanwhile, back to Andy.

– Thanks very much Nick . . .

Section 4

Tasks 2 and 3   (1′46″)

. . . And we have a caller on Line 2, now; Mr. Jackson from Bolton, who, I believe, wants to talk to Norman about setting up a dark-room. Are you there, Mr. Jackson?

Er, yes. Well, er actually, it's about er colour-developing at home, really . . .

– So, there we are. Our four contestants are ready and waiting, here in the studio, to pit their wits against each other and the mighty Oxford English Dictionary. And one of them will be going through, after today's round, to do battle in the first semi-final, in three weeks' time.

– . . . And after about twenty minutes, on a medium heat at the bottom of your oven, it should come out with the cheese nicely melted and browned over those slices of egg on the top.

Next week I'll be giving you some tips about freezing your summer fruit for the winter. So, I hope you can join me. Until then, goodbye.

– We've got a high of nine degrees Celsius, forty-eight degrees Farenheit, with rain closing in from the west and that should be covering all of our area by lunch-time. So, if you're out this morning, you'd better take an umbrella with you.

– O'Keefe played a brilliant match. He headed a corner from Rainer, just two minutes before the final whistle, which bounced off the post and had the United goalkeeper, Stevenson, in a bit of a panic for a few moments, before the new boy, David Briggs, came through, like lightning, to clear the ball out of the area. United 2: Villa 1.

Section 5

Task 2 (2′51″)

– An inquest has been opened into the deaths of eleven flying enthusiasts who were killed (when their plane crashed) in Cheshire. The hearing heard that the aircraft was given (an official inspection), which it passed, only days before the tragedy. Denise Shaw has been at the inquest:

– The 32-year-old Vickers Varsity (was bought by) the Nottinghamshire Aircraft Preservation Society in 1978. The enthusiasts restored the plane and regularly (took it to air-shows) all over Britain. They were on their way to Blackpool when the aircraft (developed engine-trouble) and crashed, near Northwich, ten days ago. Three men survived the crash, eleven died. This morning the inquest was told that the dead had been identified by (dental records and personal effects). Civil Aviation Authority experts had only certified the doomed plane as airworthy (days before the crash). The inquest was adjourned until investigations into the tragedy are completed by the Department of Transport.

– An inquiry is to be held into the collision between a passenger ferry and a Belgian cargo ship (off the French coast). The collision, which happened yesterday afternoon in fog, caused the Belgian ship to sink, but the ferry, the Panorama Voyager, (was only slightly damaged). She set sail, once again, this morning from Southampton. Alan Lomas reports:

– Less than twelve hours after the accident the Voyager left Southampton bound for Santander in Spain. The ferry was examined by maritime surveyors and (pronounced seaworthy) after she'd arrived in Southampton last night. Her owners, Panorama Lines, say the Voyager has nothing more than cosmetic damage and they haven't yet decided when she'll (be taken out of service) for repairs. A waitress aboard the Voyager said she thought (the Belgian vessel), the Esprit de Coeur, was going to be cut in half and a passenger said he couldn't believe his eyes when (he went up on deck) to see what had happened. The crew of the Esprit de Coeur were all transferred to rescue tugs before the two ships were towed apart. (There were no casualties) from either ship. The inquiry will start next week.

– There has been a collision between a passenger train and a goods train in Greater Manchester. The goods train was (carrying fuel oil) and some of its tankers exploded and (burst into flames) in the accident. The fire has now been put out by foam. First reports say that two people have been killed. The accident happened on a stretch of line which runs close to a residential area in Salford and a section of the M602 motorway, (alongside the track), has been closed to traffic to allow emergency services to (get to the scene). There are reported to be about seventy people injured, but only four of them seriously. The passenger train, the 11:07 service from Liverpool to Leeds, had just passed through the station at Eccles when (it ran into the back) of the goods train. British Rail have refused to comment on speculation that (a signals failure) was the cause of the accident. They say their investigators will begin work immediately. Police have issued the following telephone number (for information about the crash): that's . . . 061 228 2973.

Section 5

Task 3 (2′51″)

(The listening text for Task 3 is the same as for Task 2 except that the words in brackets are replaced by the numbers 1–7 in each bulletin.)

UNIT 6

Section 1

Task 1 (0′33″)

Richard Penject is er . . . it's like a James Bond syringe it's . . .

Interviewer Novo Pen

Richard Yeah, Novo Pen, getting the brand name. Plug for the pen. It's like er it's like a biro or a fountain pen which you can twist the top off and it turns into a syringe and I mean it just means the amount of flexibility you've got just carrying it around you can just put it in your pocket, walk down the street and then if you wanna stop and do an injection you can. You can go into restaurants and do it without people even looking at you. It's brilliant, really good.

Section 1

Task 4 (3′29″)

Interviewer Richard, you're one of Virginia's patients, [That's right] Erm how did you first know that you had diabetes?

Richard Erm I was on a camping holiday with my parents and my mother had recently read an article in a woman's magazine which described the symptoms which are desperate thirst and also urinating a lot. And, er because we were camping, my mother filled up the water buckets for the morning the night before and er she realized one morning that she'd filled two 2-gallon buckets and found only half a bucket left in the morning, so I'd drunk 3 gallons of water during the night and of course urinated it all out as well. It was quite soggy round the tent!

Interviewer Good heavens! And did you feel ill?

Richard Yeah, you feel really ill, you feel like very thirsty, really thirsty and sweating a lot and just tired, lethargic, you can't do anything.

Interviewer So she then took you off to the doctor, did she?

Richard Yeah, where . . . to a GP who did a urine test which was the standard way of testing for diabetes and of course I . . . my sugar content was sky high; and that's an automatic sign really that you're diabetic.

Interviewer And how old were you when all this happened?

Richard I was 5½.

Interviewer So are those symptoms common? Is that what everybody suffers from? This thirst?

Virginia Yes on the whole . . . I mean . . . when erm well put it this way, your body needs sugar erm to function, just you know for sleeping, working, playing, all those sorts of things. And it's insulin that erm enables your body to use the sugar, and so if you haven't got enough, the sugar builds up in the blood and you actually get . . . well in fact you get dehydrated really and the only way your body can get rid of the sugar is to send it out through the kidneys, through the urine. So you send out loads and loads of urine and so you get this awful thirst and so that . . . that's usually the first symptoms, especially with somebody young you know who's going to actually need insulin.

Interviewer So what's the treatment now for diabetes?

Virginia Well it . . . I mean it depends when and sort of how you get diabetes. If . . . on the whole, below the age of erm about 30, you're going to need to have insulin injections for the rest of your life because you're, you're not producing . . . you're just not producing enough insulin and probably no insulin after a while. But erm there are lots . . . it's almost what 2% of the population, possibly more, now have diabetes and in the sort of the later age range people develop it um and sometimes it can be controlled just by diet or with diet and tablets.

Interviewer And the effect on people's diet, does it vary for each individual, or are there basic rules that all diabetics follows?

Virginia What you advise for diabetes now is um the diet that you recommend for everybody, you know, that you have um plenty of fresh vegetables and fruit, and um enough carbohydrate to fill you up um and preferably sort of high fibre carbohydrate, and um cut down on fats, which . . . it's actually the opposite almost that you were recommended, what 10 years ago.

Section 2

Task 2 (1'18")

Interviewer I understand you're interested in holistic medicine. Can you explain what holistic medicine is?

Vivienne OK. Holistic medicine, um, takes into consideration the whole of the person. Now what this means in, in most holistic systems is regarding the person as a physical entity, a mental or emotional person, and also even their spiritual side of them. Um, it also includes looking at the body as a whole rather than looking at individual parts of the body, and as a way of explaining this, we could look at conventional medicine as producing people who are like a cardiologist, who looks at a heart, um, a brain specialist, a person who deals with bones, er, etc. So what we've tended to do in conventional medicine is break things down to a point where we're actually only looking at one part of the person and we're not actually relating terribly well that part to the rest of the body, whereas holistic medicine insists that if there is a problem, er, with your right foot, that is going to somehow, um, affect your entire body.

Section 2

Task 5 (2'23")

Interviewer Um, your speciality is acupuncture. Er, is that a part of holistic medicine?

Vivienne Acupuncture is very much a holistic system. Um, traditionally the Chinese regarded the person very much as a whole entity and acupuncture itself works on an energy system basically, and in a very simplified way, it's saying that, er, you have an energy system within your body and when that energy becomes blocked or tainted in some way, then you will manifest certain symptoms and the things that we look at in conventional medicine as things like arthritis or rheumatism are, to the Chinese, merely an imbalance of the energy. So, in this way, they may say to you, well, yes, you have rheumatoid arthritis but we're going to actually look at your energy balance and rebalance you, and, as a result, your symptoms should disappear.

Interviewer Um, is acupuncture essentially a form of preventative medicine?

Vivienne Traditionally, it was, very much. Um, in fact, traditionally, in China, people only used to pay the doctor while they were well and they used to go to their doctor fairly regularly on, you know, maybe four or five times a year, and they would only pay the doctor when they were kept well. And if they got sick, they didn't pay the doctor. And the doctor had various methods of which acupuncture was one, diet was another, exercise was another, er, of ensuring that the person lived a right life style and their emphasis was on if you're living a right life style, if you're living in tune with the laws of the universe, going to sleep when it's dark, waking up when it's light, working, resting, doing all these things properly, then you won't get sick. Unfortunately, our way of looking at life in the West is very different in that we tend to struggle on in spite of our headache and not take terribly much notice of our body when things are not quite right and we tend to struggle on until we fall over and we get carted off to hospital in an ambulance. And so, acupuncture in the West, unfortunately, in a way, has come to be not the preventative medicine that it could be because we're not taking responsibility enough for ourselves in going along and making sure that we stay well.

UNIT 7

Section 1

Tasks 3 and 4 (3'58")

Interviewer Like me, you've probably always believed that diamonds—those gorgeous, brilliant, shining jewels—are precious because they're both beautiful and rare. It's the demand for rare gems that makes them expensive. Well, the author of *The Death of the Diamond* is an American writer and journalist, Edward J. Epstein and, when I met him in his apartment in New York earlier this year, he soon put me right on a few things.

Edward Epstein Diamonds are not rare at all. They're one of the most common minerals in the crust of the earth. In fact, if you think about it, there are more diamonds in America, or England, than any other commodity, except for a television set. There are more diamonds than cars. There are more diamonds than families with children. There are more diamonds than dishwashers or other appliances. Almost every family, at least in America, has a diamond.

Interviewer If that's so, why is it that diamonds should be so expensive?

Edward Epstein Well, diamonds are expensive because there's a monopoly that has tried to fix the price of diamonds and they charge a rent for getting married. It's a marriage rent. Because you think it's symbolic and important for the marriage, you're willing to buy a little pebble, that you wouldn't buy in a store if you weren't getting married, and pay $1000. It's sort of a private marriage licence.

Interviewer Edward Epstein's book is an exposé of that monopoly. The corporation in question is De Beers; the South African company that exercises extraordinary control over the world's diamonds. There are many strange and unexpected twists to the story. For instance, diamonds are found in many places in the world; there have recently been big finds in Australia, for example. But, De Beers' main suppliers outside South Africa are, surprisingly, the Russians and, as is better known, Black African states, such as Zaire, Angola and Tanzania. De Beers' policy for dealing with these unlikely allies is very simple:

Edward Epstein De Beers makes an offer to buy up all the diamonds in the world at a set price. And, because it controls the means of cutting, the means of distribution, the means of credit and financing for diamonds, most African countries find it worthwhile to sell to De Beers. De Beers then puts it all in a central stockpile and then redistributes it to the diamond cutters in Belgium, in England and other, Israel, and other places.

Interviewer It seems quite extraordinary to think that Black African nations, which are, presumably, pledged to the downfall of South Africa should have this constant arrangement with a South African corporation.

Edward Epstein Well, it's one of the many ironies of the diamond business (is) that South Africa is, in a sense, dependent on Black Africa, especially Zaire, not to compete with it. But I have a feeling that this relationship goes deeper than merely diamonds; that South Africa is an important economic force in all of southern Africa.

Interviewer Does that mean that De Beers has political power within the Black African states?

Edward Epstein Er, not necessarily, because it's really, purely, as they say in *The Godfather*, a business

relationship. They buy diamonds that countries couldn't sell elsewhere. It's very hard to sell diamonds because people think of diamonds as these beautiful crystals they see on people's fingers, but, when they come out in a rough state, they're all shapes, all forms, all sizes. And they all have to be cut and there are very few specialist cutters in the world; and De Beers controls most of them. So, what do you do if you're the country of Tanzania and you have a pile of these little stones? Who do you sell them to? De Beers makes the best offer.

Interviewer You've mentioned "The Godfather" talking about the relationship between South Africa and these Black African states. That suggests it's a pretty sinister kind of relationship.

Edward Epstein I think that it's sinister only in the sense that it's concealed and secretive. There might be some bribes that go on to leaders of African countries to sell the diamonds cheaper, but I think you have to look at it as, basically, a business relationship. How else could they sell these tiny pebbles, that have no real intrinsic value, to America and Japan, except through De Beers; that knows how to cut 'em, market 'em and, mainly, inflate the price through advertising and trickery.

Section 2

Task 2 (1′15″)

Edward Epstein Basically, it has a problem. And that is only so many people get married every year. Well, they had one market that just came along naturally, and that was America. In America people didn't know what they were supposed to do when they got married. We're talking about the beginning of the twentieth century. They had no tradition, so they accepted the diamond tradition. De Beers had great problems finding other countries in the world and, after the War, actually in 1963 or '64, began looking at Japan. And it saw that the main motive of the Japanese was to be more like Westerners and less like Asians. They wanted to be part of the modern world. And taking, working on this assumption, De Beers designed an advertising campaign which identified giving a diamond as a passport to being a Westerner, to being a modern, er, man. And they found enormous response in Japan. And Japan, where there was no diamond tradition. There wasn't even a tradition of giving any er precious stone. It went from practically zero to 65% in about six years. And now in Japan, which is De Beers' second largest market to the United States, and where maybe 25% of the diamonds are sold, they have an established market. It's absolutely miraculous.

Section 3

Task 2 (2′04″)

Interviewer One other advertising campaign that people will always think of in connection with the diamond is 'A Diamond is Forever.' Where, where did that idea come from? Who invented that slogan?

Edward Epstein Well, the slogan was coined by an American advertising agency called N. W. Ayer but the important thing is what it suggests and this is why I use the world trickery. It suggests to people that the value of the diamond is for ever. Infact, not even a diamond is for ever, because if you heat it over a flame, or something, it'll turn black and shatter. But that's not going to happen, but what, in people's mind they think if they invest in a diamond they always have that diamond that they can turn back into the money they spent; which is completely untrue. You can never get your money back for a diamond, when you take inflation out of the picture. Of course, the moment you buy it the store is taking a profit of maybe 40 or 50% and the distributor and everyone else. So, you would have to wait maybe 10 or 20 years before you ever even equalled your money. Er, and it's very unlikely you would. And a diamond has such sentimental value, which is another part of the genius of De Beers; (is) identifying a sentimental value with a business transaction. So people are conflicted: On one hand, they've bought a diamond because they thought it was an investment. On the other hand, it has great sentimental value to them.

Interviewer So, this is part of the clever thing, that, if De Beers is trying to control the, the supply of diamonds onto the market, if someone's bought a diamond "forever," or if a diamond is a girl's best friend, the diamond is not going to be resold. And, therefore, the market is, in theory, not going to be flooded by all the diamonds that have already been bought by individuals.

Edward Epstein Yes, that's, that's true. Every diamond ever sold since the beginning of time is, really, the above-the-ground inventory of diamonds and it's maybe a hundred times the production from the mines. If people suddenly decided to sell their diamonds there would be no buyers for them and the diamond market would collapse. So, it's very important for De Beers, as long as it's going to continue the illusion, to continue sentimentalising diamonds. Because, the moment the sentiment's gone, diamonds just become another little pebble, like rubies, or anything else.

UNIT 8

Section 1

Task 1 (0′44″)

Barrie Well ＿＿＿＿＿＿ funnily enough go to dances if you like, and when a male er meets a female in the air they actually put on their best perfumes and aftershaves. These are pharamones of course, because ＿＿＿＿＿＿ give off this wonderful pharamone, this aroma, which does attract each other. In fact they are used in human perfumes as well. Now when they go and meet in the air they actually have a little dance, and they dance together there, and if he's not a very good dancer and treads on her toes or he doesn't smell quite

right, then she'll reject him and she'll go off and dance with another fella 'til she finds the right one. That works both ways too. And then whilst they've danced together in the air and if they like each other they then go down and join together and and remain mated for perhaps a couple of hours. So they're not like unlike us really. They're very complicated creatures and we can learn a lot from them I think.

Section 1

Task 5 (1′55″)

Interviewer Barrie, can you tell me what exactly is a butterfly farm?

Barrie Butterfly farm is a place where we er collect exotic butterflies by buying them in from all parts of the world – in the chrysalis stage by the way – not actually buying adult butterflies – and they are allowed to hatch and release into a tro- tro- tropical environment which is very realistic to what you might see somewhere in South America or the Far East, where they can fly about and live freely and people can experience them – this is the paying public – can come in and experience them flying around freely as they would in the wild.

Interviewer Hmm. Well wh what does it look like? I mean what what would it look like inside? Can you describe the building and the inside of it? [Yes]

Barrie Basically I suppose you might say it was a greenhouse, but we don't like to call it that, we call it a butterfly house. Er they're normally around 8000 square feet in size, and as you walk in through the door you get the smell straight away of the flowers. It's very humid and damp, just as it is under the secondary jungle canopy. And er you'll find there's lots of dripping plants: bananas, bougainvilleas, lantanas, all sorts of exotic flowers and plants, which the caterpillars can eat, and the butterflies can feed on. And as you walk around you'll experience large ponds with beautiful lilies in them. I've got er one called the Star of India which is very beautiful, a lovely big blue one, which is also good for nectar for butterflies. And as you go further round you'll see all sorts of little er bits and pieces, birds, all sorts of things, it isn't actually just butterflies nowadays, we've taken it further.

Interviewer What's the purpose of a butterfly farm? What's it for?

Barrie Yeah, the purpose of a butterfly house is to give people the experience of nature close at hand. Something that is a very modern idea and is coming more and more round . . . zoos eventually will go this way. So that you actually come much closer to the reality, rather than behind bars or behind glass. It's not just for the experience for the public, it's also for us to do a bit of research to find out more about these creatures. I'm actually making the er unit available for universities and such like to use this facility so that they can come in and study for themsevles. So it's got two functions.

Section 2
Tasks 1, 2 and 3   (8′08″)
Interviewer   Can you tell me something about the different families of butterfly?

Barrie   Yes, there are fifteen families of butterflies altogether in the world. And we're going to choose just a few of these today I think. And they come in all varying shapes and sizes and although they're put into family groups because of their shape sometimes, but also it's because of their behaviour and their type of environment which is all er important to the way that they are categorized in their families. They're in fact still being moved around today. I I just about learn a new species, and they suddenly move it into a new family, so it's still very complicated.
(0′32″)

Interviewer   Right there's erm something called erm the owl butterflies. What family do they belong to?

Barrie   Well the owl butterfly comes from a group of butterflies called brassolidae. They're very beautiful butterflies. They're quite large: they can have wing spans of 9 or 10 inches. Normally they're of a very dark brownish colour on the outside of the wing with this wonderful big eye on the wing, hence the name owl butterfly. But some of them when they flash open their wings are electric blue, and are really quite magnificent. And when they're seen flashing around at dusk – because they're crepuscular – they are a magnificent sight.

Interviewer   What do they eat?

Barrie   Right, well they eat . . . you mean by the eat is the caterpillar? . . . the caterpillar actually eats the banana plant. Banana is a very important plant to this species because it also . . . the adult only feeds on rotting bananas. And of course you can imagine that this probably could be a pest in South America, and in Brazil is becoming so.
(0′49″)

Interviewer   What about the monarch butterfly?

Barrie   The monarch butterfly is a very famous butterfly, well publicised because of its long migration up and down the United States . . . well in fact from Canada down to Mexico. But what is unique about him is – well not unique actually – he comes from a family of butterflies that are in fact very poisonous, [Mmm] and their colours show you this. They are bright orange with black striping, which is always a distasteful marking, and birds know to avoid.

Interviewer   What's the family called?

Barrie   The family's called Danidae. [Uh huh] Right, now he feeds on a plant called the milkweed – acclepis cassavica – for Latin lovers – which is a very poisonous plant, and the caterpillar eats this and retains all these poisons in his body, and when he pupates and goes through the metamorphosis, gives it to the adult as well.

Interviewer   And where where do they live?

Barrie   Well in fact this is a very successful butterfly. It lives all up and down the States – you can see them all through the year at different times and areas – and in fact they've now colonized South America, Central America, right across the other side down in Australia, New Zealand, even up in the Canary Islands now. Who knows, they may be in Britain and Europe before we know it!
(1′03″)

Interviewer   Heliconidae, that's another family, isn't it? What what are they?

Barrie   Heliconius, are a very interesting er species of butterflies. There are seventy different species in this family. They're very distinctive by their shape of wing: they have long narrow wings. And they're a very cheeky little flier, because again they're rather distasteful, rather poisonous. And they flitter around you very cheekily, they're not frightened of anything, because they're not going to be eaten by birds. They're very brightly coloured – stripes black and white or with orange or with red – and they feed on a plant called passion flower which is obviously a very well-known plant around the world, and er these occur in central South America, although there is one species that just occurs up into Florida.
(0′37″)

Interviewer   Can you say something about swallowtails?

Barrie   Swallowtails – well everybody's heard of a swallowtail. This is the one that sticks in everybody's mind – if you ask them what butterfly do they like, they'll always say a swallowtail. Swallowtails can be very large or very small. Some of them have very long tails, hence the name. They have very attractive colourations again, all the colours of the rainbow. In fact they're probably the most diverse of all the butterfly families that we're going to talk about. But it gets more complicated than this, because some swallowtails don't have any tails at all. Then you get kite swallowtails which have the shape of a kite. And then you get little ones like the dragon-tails they're called, which come from the Far East, they they have very small wings but all tails, so it becomes very complicated indeed, and so these need looking at very much more closely so that you can find out what family they belong to.

Interviewer   And what sort of habitat do they live in?

Barrie   Well they occur in all sorts of habitats throughout the world: in deep jungle, on top of the jungle canopy, in open temperate areas, marshland, and they feed on a variety of plants – our English swallowtail feeds on the plant called fennel, [Mmm] fennel which is er grows in sort of damp areas naturally in the wilds. But a lot of exotic swallowtails, especially in the Far East, feed on citrus, the orange trees, lemon trees and such like. And of course again you can imagine that these can be pests. There are quite a few pest species in the world.
(1′18″)

Interviewer   In Britain we have a lot of white butterflies. What what family do they come from?

Barrie   Yes, the whites come from a family called

Pieridae. And the Pieridaes are always whites or yellows – we call them sulphurs. And these are bright . . . are very white coloured because they live out in the open. White colour butterflies reflect excessive light so as they don't overheat. So this is why you always see cabbage whites out in the fields and in your gardens devastating your cabbages,

Interviewer Are they only found in Britain?

Barrie No, they're found throughout the world. There are cabbage whites all over the world, so they just occur and don't plague us – they do occur everywhere. (0′33″)

Interviewer What about the the blues? What er . . .

Barrie Now that's the lycaenids or lycaenidae. These are normally smallish butterflies. They have very interesting little quirk of girating their hind wings. They're also not just the blues. We also call them the hairstreaks as well. And these can occur in all sorts of habitats: up in the trees or on meadows. They're very bright colours again, can be – but this time they can be bright greens, er blues, reds, oranges . . . and although these are not distasteful, they do hold very bright colours sometimes. And they have . . . a lot of these species actually have long tails as well, little wispy tails. Very attractive butterfly. (0′35″)

Interviewer Can you say something about the morphs of South America?

Barrie The morphos yes. [Morphos] These are beautiful butterflies. I'm afraid these are used in making trays and toilet seats and all sorts of strange objects, because of their electric blue wings. This iridescence is so striking, that people fall in love with it whenever they see it, and it's made into jewellery. They are very very large butterflies again, very similar in size and shape to the owl butterfly: when his wings are shut, almost the same colour, but when their wings are open, the blue far outweighs the blue of the owl butterflies. And their sheer size. Some of these can be as large as 12 inches. 300 millimetres or 30 centimetres.

Interviewer And they're only found in South America?

Barrie Yes, these are only found in central South America [central], nowhere else in the world. (0′43″)

Interviewer In Venezuela though we had in the garden erm a butterfly that used to crackle about. We used to call them crackers. Can you – what family do they belong to?

Barrie Yes, this is a very large family. The family's called Nymphalidae. And Nymphalidae again are a very diverse family. Again occurring in all colours, shapes and sizes. Now the cracker butterfly which you can probably imagine, er makes a very strange sound and he actually is able to crackle, make this lou . . . noise like static electricity I suppose you might describe it. Whenever he's er chasing off a rival or attracting a mate. And we don't yet know how this is done. We've

had experiments done on this and originally it was thought that they actually rubbed their wings together to make static electricity, but we've now disproved this, so it's one of these unknown things in science. Hopefully we'll find out. He's not a very big butterfly: he's got about a 3½ inch wing span, but he has the most beautiful detailed markings, very intricate, not brightly coloured, but lovely gentle blues and greys. He's . . . I think he's one of my favourite butterflies.

Interviewer Hmm, what about the leaf butterfly? Doesn't that belong to the same family?

Barrie Yes it does. The leaf butterfly again is very descriptive, and when his wings are shut . . . well let me explain something. Er Nymphalid species are very good at defending themselves. Sometimes in two different forms. When their wings are shut they actually look very well camouflaged, and the leaf butterfly, not only does he look like a leaf when his wings are shut, but he has the little stem of the leaf, and when he roosts at night he sits upside down with his little stem and his tails on the branch. So he looks like a leaf hanging on the branch. And he even sways gently like a leaf blowing in the breeze. To me that's an amazing way of defending yourself. But, if he's still found and disturbed, he then flashes open his wings and he's got the most vivid orange stripes and blue, iridescent blue again, inside to just frighten away perhaps the predator at that last moment. So he's very clever at defending himself. Also of course these bright colours inside are to find a mate – we must remember that – that's so they can identify with one another. When they sit with their wings shut probably a mate wouldn't be able to find him or her anyway. (1′58″)

Section 3

Task 2 (1′58″)

Interviewer Can you say something about the problems that butterflies are having in the countryside today? What's happening in the countryside and why butterflies are becoming perhaps scarcer?

Barrie Yes, I think that's the correct word, they're becoming scarcer. They're not necessarily rare yet, although there is an exception to that: the large blue is a very good species to talk about.

But as far as why they are are becoming scarcer: we can't blame the farmer all the time, it isn't all his fault. We blame pesticides and such like. Well actually it's herbicides more than pesticides because herbicides were put down to kill off all the wild weeds and flowers so there's more grass for them to graze. And of course, it's the wild flowers that the butterflies feed on. Insecticides are basically used on the fields that are ploughed anyway. And there's no butterflies going to live there, although they do get into the hedges a little bit. But that's only very minor.

We're all responsible: the concrete jungle, our beautiful gardens with our lawns and our rose beds sprayed with everything we can imagine. What poor old butterfly can live there? He wants a few wild flowers, some stinging nettles and a few nice buddleias. So yes, we're all responsible.

Interviewer And what can ordinary people do to try and help butterflies?

Barrie Even if you've only got a very small garden, you can do your own bit really. Is to have a little corner perhaps down the back, and you don't even have to look at it, hide it if you don't like it too much, neighbours will always complain, but tell them that they haven't got one and then perhaps they'll want one themselves and that is to grow buddleias of course.

Buddleias are very good nectar for butterflies. Doesn't have to be the blue one either, the purply blue one, there are all sorts of colours, white's just as good. But you want to grow a few stinging nettles behind that, hide them behind the buddleia. But er obviously nobody likes stinging nettles but there are four species in this country that rely upon that for their survival – we must have them.

But it isn't again . . . comes back to the wild flowers. Instead of having all lawn, have a nice little circular area and seed it with some wonderful wild flowers: kidney vetch, trefoils, cornflowers, corn cockles for your own pleasure, because they're lovely colours. Very rare some of these flowers now. And you'll find that you don't need to introduce butterflies, they will just occur. Suddenly little blues will start to appear in your little meadow, browns, and several other species. It's a wonderful experience, and people should do this.

UNIT 9

Section 1

Tasks 2 and 3 (2'03")

1 We eat an early lunch and drink some more champagne, looking down at the Austrian Alps.

2 Three hours after taking off, we're on the ground in Egypt. We straggle past the armed soldiers who guard Cairo Airport and climb into three coaches.

3 We started drinking free champagne in the special Concorde Departure Lounge at the airport and now excitement is high.

4 The Pyramid of Cheops was considered as one of the Seven Wonders of the World and it was built by 100,000 men.

5 Nearly everyone has a camera and, already, they're taking pictures of each other, of the stewardesses, of the sky outside the window.

6 Yeah. I really believe I'm here now. Yeah, I've seen a Pyramid and I've seen a camel and I'm riding on it.

7 . . . and then we were back, once more on Concorde for another supersonic journey, more champagne, another meal, another chance to visit the flight deck.

8 We seem to be airborne amazingly quickly; climbing steeply away into the morning sky.

9 We all hope that you've had a very, very pleasant day and, also that we'll see you again.

10 Er, we're now just heading towards our last turn, which will be a right hand turn towards Cairo. And, just before that, we'll be starting to slow up.

11 Buses packed solid with people; a face pressed against the glass, here and there, watching us silently as we glide by in our air-conditioned comfort.

Section 2

Tasks 2 and 4 (4'03")

a

Woman Oh, I think it's great. I think it's absolutely fantastic.

Interviewer Just to think – a few hours ago we were in England.

Woman Yeah. I really believe I'm here now. Yeah, I've seen a Pyramid and I've seen a camel and I'm riding on it.
[English?
That's right.
Yes.
Welcome.
Thank you.
Thank you.]

Interviewer What was the main reason for coming on this trip?

Woman The first reason was because I wanted to fly in Concorde and the other reason was that I wanted to see the Pyramids and the Sphinx. Some people thought I was crazy, but a lot of people are very envious. They would like to have come as well.

Interviewer Are you very wealthy, or have you just saved up?

Woman I retired from teaching last year and I'm spending part of my lump sum. I decided I was going to enjoy my money while I, while I could.

b

Woman Absolutely overwhelming. You can't make any comparison with a ordinary aircraft and the Concorde. Never want to fly again ordinary after this, at all.

Interviewer Is the flight on Concorde the main reason you're here, or is . . .?

Woman Yes it is. Yes, definitely. It's an ambition and an indulgence. I've always wanted to do it and now I've done it and it's absolutely great.

Interviewer Do you have friends at home who think you're barmy just to spend all this money for a day, when, for the same money, you could go to Florida for three weeks?

Woman Of course there are, but they don't have any erm, they don't have any idea. If they had this experience they'd know it was worth it. You know you're on Concorde. It lifts you high. It's everything it should be.

c

Interviewer It's fantastic. We've flown on Concorde and you've ridden on a camel all in the same day.

Man From one extreme to the other.

Interviewer What's the most important part of today for you? Was it the flight on Concorde? Is that really what makes it worthwhile?

Man Yes, that's what I came for really.

Interviewer Are there friends who say you're barmy, spending all this money just for one day out?

Man No, they're all envious – Goodbye, yeah – and I think it's been worth every penny up to now – Goodbye. [I hope you'll come next time. Thank you.]

d

Man Today was a normal take-off. I didn't notice we were taking off at all. Er usually, your ears start to pop, er, you have a tre, tremendous impression of noise, but this was very quiet. My friends at home have no idea of how much money I'm spending just for one day.

Interviewer Do you think it's worth it?

Man Oh, of course it is. Last week my wife went to Harrods and she spent about £1,000 in all the departments in Harrods. And, this week, I'm doing the same sort of thing by going out for the day on Concorde.

e

Man Well, I've been on an ordinary plane and, er, well I've never liked flying, but this this flight, really, is has put me quite at ease, as as well as the champagne, which you don't normally get on the ordinary flight.

Interviewer If you've never liked flying . . .

Man What am I doing here? Yes. Well, I've come with my father, actually, who, who fancied the idea and I thought, er, 'Yes. Well, why not? Let's go.' You know, I can go in, go into work Monday and, er, start talking to people and say, er, 'Yeah. Well, I thought the Pyramids looked quite nice!' And things like this, you know. It's a bit of, er, one-upmanship, really, isn't it?

Interviewer It's a very friendly atmosphere on board, too, isn't it? I was wondering when I, before I came whether it would be very wealthy, flashy people, but it's really, very, it's just ordinary people.

Man Well we, we wondered who, who was going to be on it, er, we don't consider ourselves wealthy or flashy; perhaps someone who couldn't afford to come does, but we're certainly not flashy or wealthy.

Interviewer Once-in-a-lifetime thing, isn't it?

Man That's right. I, I shan't do it again and, er, what a thing to be able to tell everyone; 'I popped over to Cairo for the day.'

f

Woman I was rather scared, erm, when the camel got to its feet, because I thought I was going to fall off. It did feel a little lop-sided. But, er, I did hear one of the, erm, gentlemen say 'If you ride with a relaxed body, let your body move with the camel.' And so I relaxed and, er, it was quite good after that. It's something I just never, ever dreamed I would do, especially at my time of life. Er, I've retired early and I thought 'Well, you know, this is it. I shall never go anywhere, or do anything very much'. I'm not an adventurous sort, but this is so fantastic; it's absolutely unbelievable. I am not a rich person, but, er, I don't think money is so important; you can't take it with you. I have no-one to leave it to and, er, you've got to get your priorities right, I think.

Section 3

Tasks 1 and 3 (3′37″)

1 Er, I enjoy it, really. Because, er, well, first of all, they pay our salary. They do enjoy looking at what they're getting and it gives them an insight in the sort of things we're doing up here and, therefore, enables them to appreciate what's going on.

2 Oh yes. We'll carry on climbing, either until we've got to decelerate the aeroplane to arrive in the Cairo F.I.R. subsonic, or until we reach a cruise altitude limit, which is 60,000 feet.

3 Er, you monitor every track change. And you've got to be fully aware of where the aeroplane is all the time in space. And you've got to know its energy profile, too. Because, for instance, to slow down it's, erm, at least a hundred miles to become subsonic. So, you've got to be completely clear in your own mind, where you are, where you're going next and what exactly the aeroplane's doing. So, although everything's automatic and it does it beautifully, you have to monitor it the whole time.

4 We're just coming up to South Crete. You'll be able to see Crete out of the left side in a moment, and you'll be amazed how quickly, infact, Crete goes past. We'll cover the length of Crete, I suppose, at the average speed of about twenty miles-a-minute. If you look down there you can see a subsonic aeroplane going the other way; which gives you some idea – Can you see it? – some idea about our speed [Oh yes]. And the closing speed of the two aeroplanes is something like 2,100 miles an hour.

5 Er, 55,700 and we're climbing very gently, because, as the aeroplane gets lighter, er, and burns off fuel, it slowly climbs and, as a result, it stays at its economical altitude at all times.

6 Well, it's . . . When they certificate an aeroplane, or when the, er, C.A.A. certificate an aeroplane, er, certain decals have got to be put up. And it's daft, of course, but, some aeroplanes you can, infact, open the D.V. window in flight; this is called a direct vision window when you can open them, er, and they're useful in, certainly older aeroplanes, if the windscreen-wipers either weren't there, or, or weren't working. But, on this aeroplane, there's a.) no requirement to open them, and, if there were, you couldn't open them anyway.

7 Oh, Crete's gone. Er, we're now just heading towards our last turn, which will be a right hand turn towards Cairo. And, just before that, we'll be starting to slow up.

8 It's always special and it's always demanding and I'd say that the only thing, – you must never relax with it, you know, you must always pay it the attention it deserves.

9 Well, first of all, I learnt to fly, er, with the Air Force as a naval pilot, because the Royal Air Force train all Navy pilots. And then I flew fixed wing fighters from the deck. Erm, then joined er B.O.A.C., as it was then, on 707's, then 7-4, still as a first officer and then

a captain on 7-0's. And then a six-month course on this aeroplane; which is fairly difficult to pass – quite demanding, but tremendous fun.

10   Well, we'd all die very quickly, because the outside air-pressure is about 1.4 p.s.i; which is the sort of pressure required to boil our blood. Erm, it's so low that, almost instantaneously, your blood would boil. The other problem is that you just could not get oxygen to your lungs. Even if one were to put on an ordinary oxygen mask, you couldn't. You'd have to use a very superior er pressure demand system; which we've got.

Section 3

Task 4   (3'21")

Where are we at the moment?

How high are we at the moment?

So we're still climbing?

Do you ever get used to flying this aircraft?

Is that really a bother, or is that something you enjoy?

And how do you get to fly a Concorde?

How much does the plane really fly itself?

Is that really necessary to have that label there?

What would happen if you could open that window?

We seem to be making a turn now. Where are we now?

Section 4

Task 2   (14'06")

Pilot   Distance to Cairo is, er, 2,500 statute miles and we've got a flight time of 2 hours and 59 minutes. We're powered by four Rolls Royce Olympus engines, which have, er, reheat, or afterburners, and, on the take-off today they should be providing us with a total of 152,000 pounds of thrust and that's equivalent to 70,000 shaft horsepower and the maximum speed the aircraft's permitted to fly at is mach 2.04; just over twice the speed of sound. Today, we'll be cruising at mach 2, precisely.

Interviewer   £795 is one heck of a lot to pay for one day out. Who on earth can afford a trip like this? Well, clearly quite a lot of people can. With 100 on today's flight, Concorde is full. It's certainly luxurious. We started drinking free champagne in the special Concorde Departure Lounge at the airport and now excitement is high as the aircraft surges forward along the runway. The first officer had told us to expect some pretty sporty acceleration on the take-off and he was right. We seem to be airborne amazingly quickly; climbing steeply away into the morning sky. I look around at the other passengers. They don't look staggeringly rich – quite like any other party of British tourists off on a package holiday, really: A high proportion of people on their own, some married couples, quite a lot of retired people. Nearly everyone has a camera and, already, they're taking pictures of each other, of the stewardesses, of the sky outside the window. What's

their first impression of flying on Concorde?

Woman   Absolutely overwhelming. You can't make any comparison with an ordinary aircraft and the Concorde. Never want to fly again ordinary after this, at all.

Interviewer   Is the flight on Concorde the main reason you're here, or is . . . ?

Woman   Yes it is. Yes, definitely. It's an ambition and an indulgence. I've always wanted to do it and now I've done it and it's absolutely great.

Interviewer   Do you have friends at home who think you're barmy just to spend all this money for a day, when, for the same money, you could go to Florida for three weeks?

Woman   Of course there are but they don't have any erm, they don't have any idea. If they had this experience they'd know it was worth it. You know you're on Concorde. It lifts you high. It's everything it should be.

Man   Today was a normal take-off. I didn't notice we were taking off at all. Usually your ears start to pop, er, you have a tre, tremendous impression of noise, but this was very quiet. My friends at home have no idea of how much money I'm spending just for one day.

Interviewer   Do you think it's worth it?

Man   Oh, of course it is. Last week my wife went to Harrods and she spent about £1,000 in all the departments in Harrods. And, this week, I'm doing the same sort of thing by going out for the day on Concorde.

Man   Well, I've been on an ordinary plane and, er, well I've never liked flying, but this flight, really, has put me quite at ease, as well as the champagne, which you don't normally get on the ordinary flight.

Interviewer   If you've never liked flying . . .

Man   What am I doing here? [Yes.] Well, I've come with my father, actually, who, who fancied the idea and I thought, er, 'Yes. Well, why not? Let's go.' You know, I can go in, go into work Monday and, er, start talking to people and say, er, 'Yeah. Well, I thought the Pyramids looked quite nice.' And things like this, you know. It's a bit of, er, one-upmanship, really, isn't it?

Interviewer   It's a very friendly atmosphere on board, too, isn't it? I was wondering when I, before I came whether it would be very wealthy, flashy people, but it's really, very, it's just ordinary people.

Man   Well, we wondered who, who was going to be on it, er, we don't consider ourselves wealthy or flashy; perhaps someone who couldn't afford to come does, but we're certainly we're not flashy or wealthy.

Interviewer   Once-in-a-lifetime thing, isn't it?

Man   That's right. I, I shan't do it again and, er, what a thing to be able to tell everyone; 'I popped over to Cairo for the day.'

Interviewer   We eat an early lunch and drink some more champagne, looking down at the Austrian Alps and then, past Venice, we accelerate and climb to twice the cruising height of any other commercial jet. Then on down the Adriatic and round into the Mediterranean at twice the speed of sound: over 1300 miles an hour. That's a mile every three seconds. Ten miles up you really can make out the curvature of the Earth and it looks even better from the flight deck, with the captain pointing out the sights.

Interviewer Where are we at the moment?

Pilot We're just coming up to South Crete. You'll be able to see Crete out of the left side in a moment, and you'll be amazed how quickly, in fact, Crete goes past. We'll cover the length of Crete, I suppose, at the average speed of about twenty miles-a-minute. If you look down there you can see a subsonic aeroplane going the other way; which gives you some idea – Can you see it? [Oh yes – some idea about our speed, yes.] And the closing speed of the two aeroplanes is something like 2,100 miles an hour.

Interviewer And how high are we at the moment?

Pilot Er, 55,700 and we're climbing very gently, because, as the aeroplane gets lighter, er, and burns off fuel, it slowly climbs and, as a result, it stays at its economical altitude at all times.

Interviewer So we are still climbing?

Pilot Oh yes. We'll carry on climbing, either until we've got to decelerate the aeroplane to arrive in the Cairo F.I.R. subsonic, or until we reach a cruise altitude limit, which is 60,000 feet.

Interviewer Do you ever get used to flying this aircraft? Is it always something a bit more special than just the kind of average aircraft that you might fly?

Pilot It's always special and it's always demanding and I'd say that the only thing, – you must never relax with it, you know, you must always pay it the attention it deserves.

Interviewer You're very generous in allowing passengers to come up and look at the flight deck. Is that really a bother, or is that something you enjoy?

Pilot Er, I enjoy it, really. Because, er, well first of all, they pay our salary. They do enjoy looking at what they're getting and it gives them an insight in the sort of things we're doing up here and, therefore, enables them to appreciate what's going on.

Interviewer And how do you get to fly a Concorde? Have you had a long career in other sorts of aircraft and now you've graduated to this?

Pilot Well, first of all, I learnt to fly, er, with the Air Force as a naval pilot, because the Royal Air Force train all Navy pilots. And then I flew fixed wing fighters from the deck. Erm, then joined er B.O.A.C., as it was then, on 707s, then 7-4, still as a first officer and then a captain on 7-0s. And then a six-month course on this aeroplane; which is fairly difficult to pass – quite demanding, but tremendous fun.

Interviewer It's so comfortable. I mean, all those old movies of pilots going through the sound barrier with their cheeks sagging and looking as though they're going to throw up.

Pilot Well, the first time I went through, I was dressed up like a spaceman, er, diving into the ground, like a lunatic, in a Hunter. Erm, tremendous fun, but you know, compared to this aeroplane, absolutely ridiculous.

Interviewer How much does the plane really fly itself and how much are you having to monitor a lot of things all the time?

Pilot Er, you monitor every track change. And you've got to be fully aware of where the aeroplane is all the time in space. And you've got to know its energy profile, too. Because, for instance, to slow down, it's, erm, at least a hundred miles to become subsonic. So, you've got to be completely clear in your own mind, where you are, where you're going next and what exactly the aeroplane's doing. So, although everything's automatic and it does it beautifully, you have to monitor it the whole time.

Interviewer One of the signs I didn't expect to see was a little label over there, I can see, that says "Do not open window in flight". Is that really necessary to have that label there?

Pilot Well, it's . . . When they certificate an aeroplane, or when the, er, C.A.A. certificate an aeroplane er, certain decals have got to be put up. And it's daft, of course, but, some aeroplanes you can, in fact, open the D.V. window in flight – this is called a direct vision window when you can open them – erm, and they're useful in, certainly older aeroplanes, if the windscreen-wipers either weren't there, or, or, weren't working. But, on this aeroplane, there's a.) no requirement to open them, and if there were, you couldn't open them anyway.

Interviewer What would happen if you could open that window? What would happen to us now if that window were open?

Pilot Well, we'd all die very quickly, because the outside air-pressure is about 1.4 p.s.i.; which is the sort of pressure required to boil our blood. Erm, it's so low that, almost instantaneously, your blood would boil. The other problem is that you just could not get oxygen to your lungs. Even if one were to put on an ordinary oxygen mask, you couldn't. You'd have to use a very superior pressure demand system; which we've got.

Interviewer Finally, when we started to talk we were just coming up to Crete. We seem to be making a turn now. Where are we now?

Pilot Oh, Crete's gone. Er, we're now just heading towards our last turn, which will be a right hand turn towards Cairo. And just before that, we'll be starting to slow up.

Interviewer Three hours after taking off, we're on the ground in Egypt. We straggle past the armed soldiers who guard Cairo Airport and climb into three coaches. Cairo is warmer than London, but not too hot at this time of the year. The traffic is horrendous. The rule of the road seems to be 'If you see a space, charge on into it before anyone else can.' Rickety lorries, piled high with baskets of tomatoes. Buses packed solid with people; a face pressed against the glass, here and there, watching us silently as we glide by in our air-conditioned comfort. Bicycles, some with two people on them. Donkey carts and a thousand cars and vans fight for every inch of the road. Six hours later, I spoke to one man, from our party, who still hadn't worked out which side of the road the Egyptians actually drive on. The guide points out the sights: The 12th century Citadel, The River Nile and, eventually, the most famous tourist sight in the world:

Guide The Pyramid of Cheops was considered as one of the Seven Wonders of the World and it was built by 100,000 men. Now, as we got very close to the Pyramid you have an included camel, or horse, or carriage ride. The ride will take you up to the second pyramid of, er, Khafre.

Interviewer Every camel driver in Egypt seems to be waiting as we get off the coach. All of them with big grins and all expecting big tips. One man I spoke to gave his driver two pounds, which was generous, but, at the end of the ride, the driver still refused to tell the camel to kneel down, so that the man could get off, until he'd given him five pounds more. I climbed into a tiny horse-drawn carriage, with a driver called Jimmy and a lady from Sussex.

Woman Oh, I think it's great. I think it's absolutely fantastic.

Interviewer Just to think – a few hours ago we were in England.

Woman Yeah. I really believe I'm here now. Yeah, I've seen a Pyramid and I've seen a camel and I'm riding on it.
[English?
That's right.
Yes.
Welcome.
Thank you.
Thank you.]

Interviewer What was the main reason for coming on this trip?

Woman The first reason was because I wanted to fly in Concorde and the other reason was that I wanted to see the Pyramids and the Sphinx. Some people thought I was crazy, but a lot of people are very envious. They would like to have come as well.

Interviewer Are you very wealthy, or have you just saved up?

Woman I retired from teaching last year and I'm spending part of my lump sum. I decided I was going to enjoy my money while I, while I could.
[This second pyramid you building by alabaster. Three million of stone of the big pyramid. Is 137 metres high. To the second pyramid . . . Tally ho! Tally ho! Welcome Egypt.]

Interviewer It was quite a ride and a good deal more comfortable, apparently, than riding up the hill on a camel.
[Thank you.]

Interviewer Well, now. How was the ride?

Man Very rough, indeed.

Interviewer And bumpy?

Man Yes. Not quite supersonic, though.

Interviewer It's fantastic. We've flown on Concorde and you've ridden on a camel all in the same day.

Man From one extreme to the other.

Interviewer What's the most important part of today for you? Was it the flight on Concorde? Is that really what makes it worthwhile?

Man Yes. That's what I came for really.

Interviewer Are there friends who say you're barmy, spending all this money just for one day out?

Man No, they're all envious – Goodbye, yeah – and I think it's been worth every penny up to now – Goodbye. [I hope you'll come next time. Thank you.]

Interviewer There's your camel – [smelly old thing!] That's the way to do it – look at that – he's racing it back down the hill to get somebody else. [Not me though.]

Woman I was rather scared, erm, when the camel got to its feet, because I thought I was going to fall off. It did feel a little lop-sided. But, er, I did hear one of the, erm, gentlemen say 'If you ride with a relaxed body, let your body move with the camel.' And so I relaxed and, er, it was quite good after that. It's something I just never, ever dreamed I would do, especially at my time of life. Er, I've retired early and I thought 'Well, you know, this is it. I shall never go anywhere, or do anything very much.' I'm not an adventurous sort, but this is so fantastic; it's absolutely unbelievable. I am not a rich person, but, er I don't think money is so important; you can't take it with you. I have no-one to leave it to and, er, you've got to get your priorities right, I think.

Interviewer In all, we had about 7 hours in Egypt. We gazed at the Sphinx; we saw a demonstration of how the Ancient Egyptians invented and made papyrus; the earliest known form of paper; we had a buffet lunch by the swimming pool at the Pyramid Holiday Inn; we went to the Bazaar – some people buying a host of souvenirs from silver and ivory jewellery to full-size camel saddles and huge brass water jugs.
As the light began to fade we stopped briefly at President Sadat's tomb and then we were back, once more on Concorde for another supersonic journey, more champagne, another meal, another chance to visit the flight deck and then, at 10.30 in the evening, just over 11 hours since we'd left England, we landed at Heathrow.

Pilot Taxiing in now to the gate. We should be there in just 2 or 3 minutes time. For those of you who collect the statistics, we were airborne for 3 hours and I think that makes it one of the quickest, if not the quickest flight back from Cairo. Maximum height was 56,000 feet. Maximum speed was 1,360 miles per hour. We, the, the crew are very proud of our Concorde and, er, it does give us a great deal of pleasure to be able to talk to you and to tell you just what we think of it. We all hope that you've had a very, very pleasant day and, also that we'll see you again. Thank you very very much for travelling with us on our Concorde. And, er, all the crew have asked me to say a special 'Good night' to you all. Thank you. Good night.

UNIT 10

Section 1

Tasks 2 and 3   (9'23")

1 In all humility, I accept the nomination . . . I am happy to be able to say to you that I come to you unfettered by a single obligation or promise to any living person.
(Thomas Dewey 24/06/48)

2 I'll never tell a lie. I'll never make a misleading statement. I'll never betray the trust of those who have confidence in me. And I will never avoid a controversial issue. Watch me closely, because I won't be any better President than I am a candidate.
(Jimmy Carter 13/11/75)

3 I am not and never have been a member of the Communist Party.
(Alger Hiss 05/08/48)

4 John Paul II, he loves you! He loves you! John Paul II, He loves you! John Paul II, he loves you! It is, it is all my message. Finished.
(Pope John Paul II 07/10/79)

5 I believe that this nation should commit itself to achieving the goal, before this decade is out, of landing a man on the moon and returning him safely to the earth. No single space project in this period will be more impressive to mankind, or more important for the long-range exploration of space; and none will be so difficult, or expensive to accomplish . . . But, in a very real sense, it will not be one man going to the moon. If we make this judgement affirmatively, it will be an entire nation . . . I believe we should go to the moon.
(John F. Kennedy 25/05/61)

6 Those of us who loved him, and who take him to his rest today, pray that what he was to us, what he wished for others will some day come to pass for all the world. As he said many times, in many parts of this nation, to those he touched and who sought to touch him: "Some men see things as they are and say 'Why?' I dream things that never were and say 'Why not?'"
(Edward M. Kennedy 08/06/68)

7 Because if they don't awake, they're going to find out that this little Negro that they thought was passive has become a roaring, uncontrollable lion right in right at their door – not at their doorstep, inside their house, in their bed, in their kitchen, in their attic, in the basement.   (Malcolm X. 28/06/64)

8 I guess I couldn't say that er I wouldn't continue to do that. because I don't want the Carter Administration, and because I don't want Secretary Vance er to have to take the blame for the decisions that I felt that I had to make, decisions which I still feel were very much in the interest of this nation, er I think it best that I remove myself from the formal employ of the government er and pursue er my interests in foreign and domestic policy as a private citizen.
(Andrew Young 15/08/79)

9 Two years ago, . . . when I landed on your soil, I said to the people of the Philippines. 'Whence I came I shall return.' Tonight, I repeat those words. I shall return.
(Douglas MacArthur 17/03/44)

10 I have a dream that one day on the red hills of Georgia, sons of former slaves and the sons of former slaveowners will be able to sit down together at the table of brotherhood. I have a dream that one day, even the state of Mississippi, a state sweltering with the heat of injustice, sweltering with the heat of oppression, will be transformed into an oasis of freedom and justice. I have a dream that my four little children will one day live in a nation where they will not be judged by the colour of their skin, but by the content of their character.
(Rev. Martin Luther King, Jr. 28/08/63)

11 Ladies and Gentlemen, you have summoned me on behalf of millions of your fellow Americans to lead a great crusade for freedom in America and freedom in the world. I know something of the solemn responsibility of leading a crusade. I have led one. I take up this task, therefore, in a spirit of deep obligation, mindful of its burdens and of its decisive importance. I accept your summons. I will lead this crusade.
(Dwight D. Eisenhower 11/07/52)

12 One thought him indestructible, so overpowering was he in his energy, warmth and his deep faith in man's inherent goodness. For 25 years he had been my friend, my older brother, my inspiration and my teacher.
(Henry Kissinger 02/02/79)

13 I have said this before, but I shall say it again, and again, and again. Your boys are not going to be sent into any foreign wars.
(Franklin D. Roosevelt 30/10/40)

14 I have never been a quitter. To leave office before my term is completed is abhorrent to every instinct in my body. But, as President, I must put the interests of America first. America needs a full-time President and a full-time Congress. Particularly at this time, with problems we face at home and abroad. To continue to fight through the months ahead for my personal vindication would almost totally absorb the time and attention of both the President and the Congress in a period when our entire focus should be on the great issues of peace abroad and prosperity without inflation at home.
(Richard M. Nixon 08/08/74)

15 In the past several months I have been living in purgatory. I have found myself the recipient of undefined, unclear, unattributed accusations that have surfaced in the largest and the most widely circulated organs of our communications media. I want to say, at this point, clearly and unequivocally: I am innocent of the charges against me.
(Spiro T. Agnew 29/09/73)

16 Our nation is moving toward two societies; one black, one white; separate and unequal.

(Otto Kerner 29/02/68)

Section 2

Tasks 2, 3 and 4 (0'59")

Dennis Morning Richard. Nasty day, isn't it? *Never rains but it pours. Lovely weather for ducks*, though.

Richard Mmm.

Dennis *Cat got your tongue*, eh? Still, *Silence is golden.*

Richard I've just heard something terrible.

Dennis *You can't believe everything you hear.* 'Course, *there's no smoke without fire* as a rule.

Richard Remember that Volvo 340DL I wanted?

Dennis *I want, never gets*, Richard. Although *everything comes to he who waits.*

Richard Yes, well. That Volvo is £415 less than the new Ford Escort 1.3GL I've just bought.

Dennis *Look after the pennies and the pounds'll look after themselves.* Of course, *you only get what you pay for.*

Richard Mmm. With a Volvo you get a safety cage, crumple zones, a heated driver's seat and I'd have saved £415.

Dennis Well, Richard, *into every life a drop of rain must fall. You've got to look on the bright side. If you didn't laugh you'd cry* and *it's an ill wind that blows nobody any good.* After all, *every cloud has a silver lining* and *it's no use crying over spilled milk*, 'cause *worse things happen at . . . (sea).*

Richard Dennis.

Dennis Yes, Richard?

Richard Shut up.

The Volvo 340DL. At only £4892, excluding number plates and delivery; *you could knock me down with a feather.*

Section 2

Task 5 (1'53")

1 I bought one of those duvets; you know to put on the bed, last Saturday. I've been saving for one for a while and I wanted a good one. Anyway, it cost me sixty-odd pounds, and, do you know what, I saw one this morning in the Co-op for less than £50. Mind you, mine's 100% duck feather and this one did have some polyester filling. But what a difference in price!

2 Look at it again. Every time I look out of that window it's raining. I don't think it's stopped raining for a week. I'm absolutely sick of it.

3 I see Nick Ashley's got married to that girl from the newsagent's. Oh, it makes me so angry, well, jealous I suppose, when I think. If only I hadn't gone with Janet to Majorca and all that business with Paco, we'd have still been going out together now. Well, it might have been my wedding last Saturday, but instead here I am with nobody . . . nothing!

4 'Ere I say, Ron. Have you heard? They say they're going to replace the five pound note with a coin, too, now.

5 What a morning! First I overslept. I don't know what happened to the alarm clock. I came running out of the house – no breakfast; jumped into the car . . . Nothing! Not a spark. Flat battery. It's my own fault, I know, but this morning of all mornings. Anyway, I saw a neighbour just coming out and managed to get a lift with her. Well, she had to drop the kids off at school first, so that made me even later. And then, to cap it all, when we got into town there's a fire in John Dalton Street . . . another half hour! It's just been one thing after another . . . Oh, no the coffee machine's broken.

Section 3

Tasks 2 and 3 (3'10")

Father says 'Never let me see you doing that again'
Father says 'Tell you once . . . tell you a thousand times.
Come Hell or high water'
His finger grills my shoulder 'Never let me see you doing that again'
My brother knows all his phrases off by heart
So we practise them in bed at night.

('Father says' by Mike Rosen)

Stepfather Ah, there you are Jane. And high time too. Where have you been?

Jane Oh, leave me alone, can't you? Why can't you mind your own business?

Stepfather It is my business, my girl. While you're living under my roof I've a perfect right to know what you've been up to when you come in at all hours of the night.

Jane You've got a right? You've got no right at all. Do you hear? You're not my father. You're nothing to do with me.

Stepfather How can you say that to me? You ungrateful girl. After all I've done for you. Don't you owe me something? Some respect, at least?

Jane Respect? I stopped respecting you when I found out how you treated my mother.

Chairman Braithwaite. Come and sit down, will you?

Eric Yes, Chairman. Thank you.

Chairman How long have you been in charge of company cars, Eric? It is Eric, isn't it?

Eric Yes, Sir, It's about seven years, Sir.

Chairman And what do you think of the Volvo, Eric?

Eric The Volvo, Sir?

Chairman Yes, the Volvo 244DL.

Eric Oh, a very nice car, Sir. A bit too pricey for our lads, if I may be so bold.

Chairman Eric, come to the window here. Is that Jenkins from Accounts I see down there getting into his new Rover 2300?

Eric I believe it is, Sir.

Chairman And were you aware, Eric, that a Volvo would have cost us less than the Rover?

Eric Oh, I . . . I . . .

Chairman And I notice, Eric, that we've recently

brought a BMW 518, a Ford Granada 2.3L. And a
Mercedes 200. All of which cost considerably more than
the Volvo.

Eric Funny how people think the Volvo costs a lot more
than it does.

Chairman We're not talking about people, Eric. We're
talking about Eric, Eric.

The Volve 244DL. At only £6,998, excluding delivery and
number plates you really ought not to pass it over.

Here is a platform change: The 18.30 service for
Portsmouth Harbour will now leave from Platform 15. The
train now standing at Platform 10 will now become the
18.17 service for Brighton, via East Croydon, Three
Bridges and Hayward's Heath. The next train to arrive at
Platform 12 will be the 17.34 service from Horsham, via
Dorking. We must apologize to passengers for the late
arrival of this service, which is due to points failure at
Clapham Junction, coupled with staff shortage, adverse
weather conditions and failure of the public electricity
supply.